Sutro's Glass Palace

THE STORY OF SUTRO BATHS

BY JOHN A. MARTINI
ILLUSTRATED BY LAWRENCE ORMSBY

HOLE IN THE HEAD PRESS
BODEGA BAY, CALIFORNIA

For information on reprinting and purchase, contact:
Hole in the Head Press
Samuel E. Stokes, Publisher
PO Box 807
Bodega Bay, CA 94923
sestokes@sonic.net
www.holeintheheadpress.com

2 3 4 5 6 7 8 9

Design: Carole Thickstun, Ormsby & Thickstun
Editor: Susan Tasaki
Indexer: Sheilagh Simpson, Bookmark: Editing & Indexing

Printed in China

Martini, John A., 1951-
Sutro's glass palace : the story of Sutro Baths / text by John A. Martini ; illustrated by Lawrence Ormsby. -- Bodega Bay, CA : Hole in the Head Press, c2014.
p. ; cm.
ISBN: 978-0-9761494-6-0
Includes index.
Summary: The story of a vanished but enduring piece of San Francisco history, illustrated with historic photographs and new artwork. Opened in 1894, the Baths contained seven swimming pools, a museum, restaurants, tropical plants, promenades, and seating for thousands; it burned in 1966. The site still attracts visitors who come to explore its concrete ruins and mysterious tunnels.--Publisher.
1. Sutro Baths (San Francisco, Calif.)--History. 2. Sutro, Adolph, 1830-1898. 3. Public baths--California--San Francisco--History. 4. Swimming pools--California--San Francisco--History. 5. San Francisco (Calif.)--Buildings, structures, etc. I. Ormsby, Lawrence, 1946- II. Title.
F869.S343 M37 2013
2013944852
979.4/61--dc23
1310

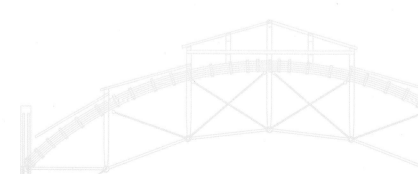

Contents

Introduction

EVERY DAY, HUNDREDS OF PEOPLE VISIT the ruins of Sutro Baths, exploring the maze of flooded foundations, concrete walls, and rocky tunnels that dot the shore and sandstone cliffs in the lee of Point Lobos.

Visitors to the little cove just north of the Cliff House are intrigued by what they see. Here, a lonely concrete pillar pokes up from a sand bank. There, the masonry foundation of what looks like a giant ice-cube tray tilts toward broken brick walls. The gaping mouth of a hand-carved cave looms in the background. In the middle, brackish water covers a network of rectangular concrete foundations, which, if the water is low and you squint hard enough, can be faintly made out through the murk.

What *was* this place?

The site is maddeningly familiar, yet indecipherable, as though a vanished civilization once flourished here at the edge of San Francisco, leaving only mysterious and flooded rubble to mark its passing.

But these are modern ruins, not an ancient archaeological site. Dating to the middle of the twentieth century, they are the weather-softened remnants of Comstock millionaire Adolph Sutro's greatest gift, and perhaps his greatest folly: the sprawling Sutro Baths & Museum.

Although it existed just seventy-two years—from 1894 to 1966—Sutro's creation left an indelible mark on the psyche of San Franciscans, both the aging locals who swam in its pools and skated on its ice rink, and more recent generations, who know the Baths only as a melancholy, broken ruin at the city's edge.

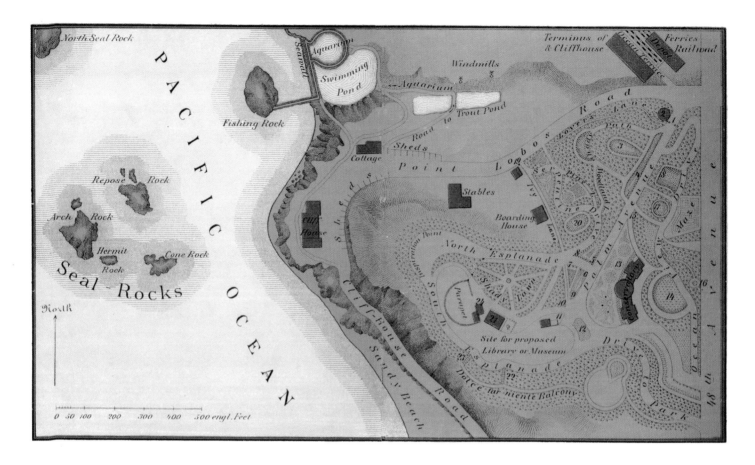

THOUSANDS OF YEARS EARLIER, the original residents of the San Francisco peninsula, the local Ohlone people, had been the first to experience the special aura of this meeting place of land and water. Then, decades before Sutro Baths was built, early American settlers began making their way to this desolate and exposed promontory, a rugged headland Spanish explorers had named *Punta de los Lobos Marinos,* or "Point of the Sea Wolves," as they called the resident sea lions of Seal Rocks. This name was eventually Yankee-ized to Point Lobos.

After the discovery of gold, San Francisco's population exploded, and residents were increasingly drawn to this westernmost part of the city to enjoy spectacular coastal views or simply to stare at the vast Pacific and the mesmerizing procession of waves crashing onto Ocean Beach.

Seal Rock Beach (the future site of Sutro Baths) and Point Lobos, circa 1884.

SPEEDSTERS RACING ON THE SANDS OF OCEAN BEACH BELOW THE CLIFF HOUSE.

During the 1850s, a tradition developed among the young city's moneyed class of riding over the dunes to Ocean Beach and onto its wet sand, which made an excellent speedway for racing all types of horse-drawn carriages—barouches, landaus, gigs, and curricles. Enterprising tavern owners soon opened roadhouses along the route so drivers and passengers could slake their thirsts: Seal Rock House, Ocean House, and, most famous of all, Cliff House. San Franciscans soon began referring to these excursions to the western shore as "going to the Cliff."

Onto this stage in 1881 strode Adolph Sutro, a newly minted millionaire, who in that year established his home on a rocky hilltop overlooking the Cliff House. While other silver and railroad barons of the era busied themselves building mansions atop Nob Hill, Sutro embarked on a program of buying up available real estate until he reportedly owned one-twelfth of the city of San Francisco.

Most of Adolph Sutro's holdings were located in undeveloped western San Francisco, and in the early 1880s, he began transforming the land surrounding his hilltop home into a series of public attractions designed to meet the recreational and cultural needs of the city's working classes. These destinations soon included a wonderfully rococo Cliff House, the landscaped gardens of his private estate at Sutro Heights, a carnival midway known as Merrie Way, a steam train and electric streetcar line bringing passengers from downtown, and the world's largest indoor natatorium—a more-than-two-acre extravaganza of stained glass, iron, and redwood that he called, modestly, the Sutro Baths.

San Francisco in the late 1800s offered few diversions for its blue-collar laborers and their families. These were the people who operated the city's factories, labored on its wharves, washed its laundry, and ran the street railways. Only a few public parks existed, most of them postage-stamp-sized plazas devoid of recreational facilities. Sutro's primary reason for constructing Sutro Baths was to provide clean, reasonably priced recreation for these folks, as well as an affordable transit system to get them there.

Sutro was not entirely motivated by altruism, however. As mentioned, the millionaire owned much of the land his patrons traversed en route to his seaside attractions, and it was all for sale. Programs for the daily events at Sutro Baths prominently displayed advertisements for Sutro's real estate agency. Once at the Cliff, visitors were engulfed in a dizzying array of attractions designed to separate them from their nickels: oyster stands, tintype galleries, waffle stands, beer joints, and, at the center of it all, the glass palace of Sutro Baths.

Adolph Sutro had developed a classic nineteenth-century business plan: create an attraction, bring visitors to it, and then sell them something.

The entrance to the four-mile-long Sutro Tunnel at the town of Sutro, Nevada. The tunnel, which ventilated and drained the Comstock mines, took nine years to complete.

Historic photographs of Sutro Baths, like this view taken by I. W. Taber circa 1895, provide important clues to understanding the complex structure.

FEW PHYSICAL POINTS of reference survive from the Baths' 1890s glory days, and historical photographs provide scant help in deciphering the present-day ruins. In order to understand the enormity and configuration of Sutro Baths, and how it once functioned, one has to pore over aging ledger books and brittle blueprints at archives around the city. It also helps to have been able to explore the building before it burned in 1966.

Like many San Franciscans, I often visited the Baths as a child to ice skate in the cavernous former bathhouse and stare with morbid wonder at the collection of Egyptian mummies, some intact and some dismembered. My curiosity was also piqued by glimpses through gaps in the painted-over windows into the closed section of the building, where I could see a labyrinth of half-drained swimming tanks and endless bleacher seats marching toward the ceiling. Sutro Baths engaged my attention at an early age, and I was fascinated by "the old barn" (as the last owner called it) long before it became today's romanticized ruin.

The mission of this book is to provide the reader with an understanding of how Adolph Sutro's magnificent glass palace was conceived by its engineer-builder; how its complex, wave-driven system of catch basins and tunnels was used to fill and drain the pools; and how the building itself was constructed, modified, and eventually reduced to ruins over the short span of seventy-two years. It is also a field guide of sorts, a way to help modern visitors understand the confusing jumble of features still surviving at the site, and give them a better appreciation of what it was like to visit the Victorian-era wonder.

ONE
Waterworks

SUTRO BATHS had its earliest incarnation as a tidal aquarium conceived by Adolph Sutro as early as 1884. Sutro had begun purchasing undeveloped land on the outskirts of San Francisco when, in March 1881, nearly on a whim, he bought a parcel of land and a tiny residence on the bluffs overlooking the Cliff House.

At first, Sutro's energies were consumed with expanding his hilltop holdings and developing his Sutro Heights gardens. Shortly thereafter, he acquired the Cliff House itself, changing its management and cleaning up the old roadhouse's seedy reputation to give it a new, family-friendly character. In short order, Sutro had embarked upon developing the Point Lobos area as a recreational destination for nineteenth-century San Franciscans.

(ABOVE) ADOLPH SUTRO IN ONE OF HIS FAVORITE POSES AS "THE HONEST MINER."
(OPPOSITE) THE CATCH BASIN AT THE TIP OF POINT LOBOS.

SUTRO ON HORSEBACK ON PALM AVENUE IN SUTRO HEIGHTS.

ADOLPH HEINRICH JOSEPH SUTRO was one of those legendary figures of nineteenth-century capitalism who could only have existed in San Francisco. At various times in his life, he was a cigar merchant, a self-trained mining engineer, builder of the fabled Sutro Tunnel that drained the Comstock Lode, owner of western San Francisco, and mayor of the city.

Born in 1830 in Aachen, Germany, twenty-year-old Sutro arrived in California at the height of the Gold Rush and began a career as a merchant in San Francisco and Stockton. In the

1850s, he started working with various mine owners and mill operators, and soon became fluent in the disciplines of mining, engineering, and ore reduction. By 1860, he was proposing a fantastical plan for digging a four-mile-long tunnel under Virginia City, Nevada, that would de-water and ventilate the deep shafts of the Comstock Lode's silver mines.

After years of political battles, fundraising, and torturous digging, the Sutro Tunnel went into operation in 1878 and was soon earning its investors $10,000 a day just for draining water from the mineshafts.

Sutro sold his interests in the tunnel a year later, just months before the Comstock silver boom went bust. Returning to San Francisco with a pile of cash, he began investing heavily in San Francisco real estate, especially along the city's undeveloped western edge.

A complex man, Sutro believed firmly in "noblesse oblige," the duty of the privileged to help the underprivileged. But his good works almost always operated on two levels. For example, Sutro purchased thousands of saplings for children to plant on the city's hillsides on Arbor Day. However, he also owned much of the land where the saplings were planted, and reaped tax credits for turning barren land into forested land.

Sutro was elected mayor of San Francisco in 1894, and quickly discov-ered that it was easier to order around Nevada silver miners than to manage San Francisco politicians. He served a single two-year term before retiring permanently to his home at Sutro Heights.

In declining health and reportedly suffering from dementia, Sutro spent his last years in his hilltop home. From his library windows, he watched the parade of visitors promenading through his Sutro Heights gardens, and visiting the Cliff House and Sutro Baths.

"THE OCTOPUS" REFERRED TO THE MONOPOLISTIC SOUTHERN PACIFIC RAILROAD.

GOLDEN GATE BY GILBERT MUNGER, 1871. AN EARLY VIEW OF POINT LOBOS AND THE MARIN HEADLANDS. (WANDA AND JAMES FISH COLLECTION)

DIRECTLY NORTH of the Cliff House lay a small, sandy beach flanked on three sides by high bluffs. Perennial hillside springs fed a brackish pond behind a barrier dune. Known variously as Seal Rock Beach or simply Point Lobos, the little beach and surrounding hillsides had been the site of seasonal Ohlone encampments for thousands of years before Europeans arrived. Sutro soon purchased the cove and the surrounding lands of Point Lobos, and enjoyed exploring its pocket beaches and tidal pools.

Sutro, never one to leave nature alone when he felt he could improve upon it, recognized the potential of turning the small cove into a visitor destination. In their 1962 book *Adolph Sutro: A Biography*, historians

Robert and Mary Stewart describe Sutro's "light-bulb moment" at Point Lobos:

> Sutro also spent hours north of Fisherman's Cove [Seal Rock Beach] watching the waves hit the rocks. There was a place where the rock was hollowed out and Adolph liked to watch a wave fill it full, and then as the waves receded, the water would gradually spill out of its little catch basin.
>
> A tide pool is a watery world whose population depends on the sea. Small fish may come and go with the waves while the more sedentary animals such as the bivalves and sea anemones accommodate themselves to the various levels of water. Here was a ready-made museum of natural history that Sutro would like to share with the public. After Papa and Mama and the little ones had visited Sutro Heights and marveled at its formal beauty, they could walk down to the ocean and see the natural garden of the sea.
>
> If only the tide pool were larger! . . . He decided that he would go into partnership with the sea and build a tide pool. Although he called it an aquarium, it was to have no roof, it would be stocked solely by the animals delivered voluntarily by the sea, and it would be filled by the waves.[1]

IN LATER YEARS, Sutro would tell reporters that he began working on his aquarium in November 1884, when he selected the site for the tide pool and catch basin and started excavations. The cove had been a tourist destination for some time, and a winding road led down from Point Lobos Avenue to the pocket beach. It had once featured a suspension bridge connecting the beach with Flagstaff Rock just offshore. The north end of the cove was already the site of a quarry, where Sutro's laborers cut stone for construction projects around his home and gardens at Sutro Heights.[2]

The earliest description of Sutro's aquarium project appeared in the *San Francisco Chronicle* in early 1886, when a reporter visited Adolph Sutro and queried him about the extensive construction going on at Point Lobos. "It is my intention to build an aquarium in that bay," replied Sutro. "It will be a saltwater aquarium entirely. It shall have in it every class of sea anemone, sea mosses, and shell fish."

But Sutro also hinted at a grander vision for the cove: "I did at first have some idea of building baths, but the rock at which I have been blasting seems to have given out, and I am afraid that I will not have enough to build a bulkhead [seawall]. . . . About the baths, my plans are in embryo. Let us first finish the aquarium. . . ." This is the first known mention of the future Sutro Baths.[3]

The aquarium itself occupied the north end of the beach, tucked into the headland that enclosed the cove on that side. Semicircular in shape, it measured roughly 100 feet by 110 feet. On the north and east sides, natural rock surfaced with concrete formed the aquarium's interior walls, while on the west and south sides, walls were constructed using a matrix of concrete mixed with rock quarried from the point. Several large natural

CIRCA 1890. THE ORIGINAL AQUARIUM IS VISIBLE AT UPPER RIGHT, AND THE NORTH-SOUTH CONCRETE SEAWALL ACROSS SEAL ROCK BEACH IS COMPLETE. A LARGE SWIMMING POND HAS STARTED TO FILL UP BEHIND THE SEAWALL.

BOULDERS QUARRIED AT POINT LOBOS PROTECTED THE CONCRETE SEAWALL FROM POUNDING WAVES.

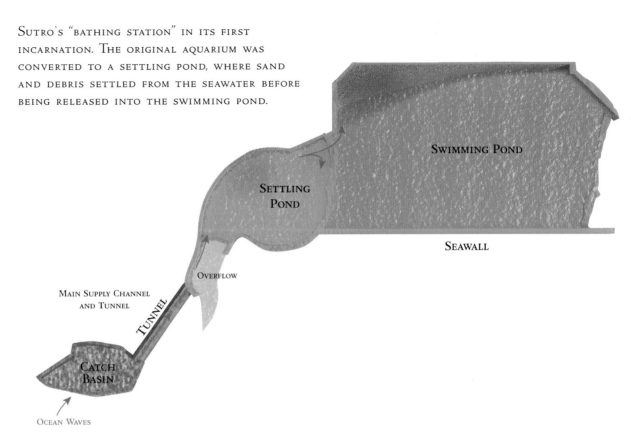

SWIMMING POND

SETTLING
POND

SEAWALL

OVERFLOW

MAIN SUPPLY CHANNEL
AND TUNNEL

TUNNEL

CATCH
BASIN

OCEAN WAVES

rocks from the beach were incorporated into the design in the hope that shellfish would continue to grow on them. Paths and stairs carved into the sides would allow visitors to descend into the drained pools.

At the tip of the bluff, about 225 feet to the west of the aquarium, sat a natural rock shelf that Sutro planned to adapt into a catch basin for the waves. Variously referred to as a "catchment," "catch water," or "ditch," the basin was intended to catch waves as they broke over the point and channel the seawater to the aquarium through a subterranean tunnel. Sluice gates would be opened to allow the water to fill the aquarium at high tide, and then closed at low tide so the water would drain away, exposing to view the marine life that would (theoretically) be tossed into the tank by wave action.

On May 1, 1887, the *San Francisco Morning Call* ran a lengthy description of the nearly complete aquarium and its workings:

> The water will come into these ponds from the ocean with fish and other marine objects in the following manner: . . . At high tide the gates will be suffered to remain open, so that the water and the living objects in it can come freely into the aquarium. At high water the whole aquarium will be flooded—the pathways and everything—and no one can go in then.
>
> The living objects will be [retained], and will seek the comparatively deep water in the ponds, and thus they will be caught as in a trap. When the waters have receded sufficiently from the pathways the public will be admitted inside the walls. Sea anemones, devil fish, angel fish . . . and perhaps even occasional seals may be caught in this aquarium. At low tide there will always be something interesting to see there.

Two weeks later, the *Morning Call* provided an update on construction at the aquarium; the writer mentioned again Sutro's vision of baths in the cove: "Mr. Sutro proposes to establish a bathing station in a cove about two acres in extent which is admirably adapted for the purpose. Of course the bathing place will be provided with all the modern improvements, and persons who are not afraid of a plunge in cold water may get a bath every day of the year."[4]

A public demonstration of the completed aquarium took place on September 3, 1887, when water first flowed through the wave tunnel and into the tank. The press corps was in full attendance, and each of the city's papers filed a story on the event. (Interestingly, none agreed on the exact dimensions of the aquarium tank, or on the length and number of tunnels through the point.) At a signal given by Sutro, construction superintendent A. O. Harrison opened a floodgate in the tunnel and a river of saltwater poured through the channels and into the aquarium. The circular pond quickly filled with 250,000 gallons of water, then the gates were closed, the drain opened, and the entire contents emptied in only six minutes. The demonstration was repeated several times for the crowd of onlookers. (If any of Sutro's hoped-for seals were washed in through the wave tunnel, no one mentioned their appearance.)[5]

Sutro took the opportunity to describe to the gathered press his growing vision for the sandy cove, which would include additional aquariums and a bathing station. As the *San Francisco Chronicle* reported, "Directly north of the Cliff House will be situated the swimming baths, which will have a graded bottom from 9 to 3 feet in depth, and will extend over two-and-a-half acres. These will be inclosed [sic] in a solid wall of masonry eight feet broad at the top."

In fact, work had already begun on sealing the entire mouth of the cove with a rock seawall in order to create the large swimming pond. According to the *San Francisco Examiner*, "The remainder of the beach of the cove, about two acres, he will then convert into a large bathing tank, which will be roofed with glass. . . ." The *Morning Call* reinforced the description: "The third and largest tank will be used as a swimming bath. This will be inclosed [sic] by an immense glass enclosure."[6]

As soon as the aquarium was completed, work accelerated on the construction of the rock seawall running the length of the cove and the creation of a swimming pond behind it. Beginning in early 1889, foreman A. O. Harrison began submitting weekly reports to Adolph Sutro on the various projects underway on and around Point Lobos. In addition to building the seawall, aquarium, and pond, his tasks included quarrying the point for rock, putting in new drains, and building an east–west seawall between Flagstaff Rock and the shore. This latter wall, called the causeway, was intended to protect the longer stone seawall from wave action.[7]

An illustration from an 1890 guidebook depicts the ongoing work at the cove during this period. The view is interesting because it shows the completed aquarium and the north–south seawall, as well as what Harrison called the "Big Pond" filling up behind it. However, there's no indication yet of the causeway connecting the seawall to Flagstaff Rock.[8]

AQUARIUM AND SWIMMING POND (HARRISON'S "BIG POND") UNDER CONSTRUCTION, 1890.

THE SAME VIEW 120 YEARS LATER. THE AQUARIUM SURVIVES AT LOWER LEFT.

A Confusion of Names

Over the years, various geographic features in and around Sutro Baths have had more than one name, the result of changing uses of the area and historical events that occurred there. For example, nineteenth-century San Franciscans called the area simply "The Cliff," but by the early 1900s, the name "Lands End" had come into use.

1. Merrie Way. Site of an amusement park assembled by Sutro from second-hand exhibits and rides from the 1894 Midwinter Fair. Alternately called Merrie Street, Midway Plaisance, and the Sutro Pleasure Ground.

2. Cliff Avenue. A steep city street descending from 40th Avenue to Ocean Beach, passing Sutro Baths and the Cliff House. Renamed Point Lobos Avenue in 1909.

3. Fisherman's Rock. A large sandstone rock located just offshore from Sutro Baths. Also historically called Flag Rock, Flagstaff Rock, and Flagpole Rock.

4. Aquarium. The semi-circular tank constructed by Sutro's workers between 1886 and 1892, originally designed to function as a giant wave-filled tide pool. Later called the settling pond when Sutro Baths was complete.

5. Point Lobos. The rocky promontory located immediately north of Sutro Baths. Alternately called Parallel Point by Sutro and his workers after the shipwreck and subsequent explosion of the dynamite-laden schooner *Parallel* at the point in 1887, an event that almost destroyed the Cliff House.

6. Catch Basin. The rock-carved basin at the tip of Point Lobos where Sutro trapped incoming waves and directed their water to the settling pond. Also called the catchment, catch water, and ditch.

TWO
The Pond Becomes the Baths

SOMETIME AROUND 1890, Sutro made a major design change by deciding to eliminate the large swimming pond. In its place, he ordered a series of interconnected concrete swimming tanks that would be filled by wave action. The technology would be an evolution of that used earlier for filling the aquarium and pond. Gone were the sea stars and devil fish; in this updated design, waves breaking at the catch basin would travel through the rock tunnel to the erstwhile aquarium, and from there, the water would be released gradually into a network of concrete channels leading to large pools of varying sizes.

There would be six pools in the new baths. The main pool would form an immense L-shape running nearly the length of Seal Rock Beach, measuring 275 feet long and 150 feet across at the dogleg. The five smaller pools were also impressive: four measured 28 feet by 75 feet, while the last was slightly larger at 50 feet by 75 feet.

Water from the former aquarium would be released into the pools via a pair of sluice gates. In this early incarnation of the Baths, there was no provision for heating or filtering the water at any point in its journey.

BY 1892, THE SWIMMING POND HAD BEEN SUBDIVIDED INTO A SERIES OF CONCRETE TANKS. AN ORNATE BOILER HOUSE RISES ADJACENT TO THE SETTLING POND.

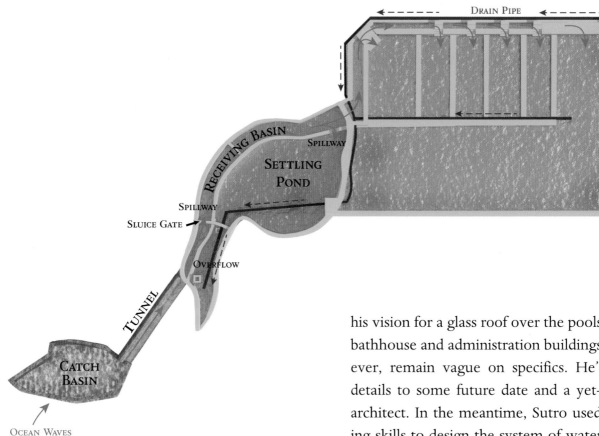

DRAIN PIPE

RECEIVING BASIN

SPILLWAY

SETTLING POND

SPILLWAY

SLUICE GATE

OVERFLOW

TUNNEL

CATCH BASIN

OCEAN WAVES

Nor was there any indication of a structure covering the tanks.[9]

Work on the concrete tanks was underway by November 1890, when foreman Harrison sent Sutro a sketch showing his progress on constructing a "N&S [North & South] Concrete Wall" 6 feet thick and 9 feet high, and running 286 feet. This wall, built just behind the existing rock seawall, would eventually form the west wall of the main swimming tank.[10] Within days, Harrison began ordering barrels of cement by the hundreds from local suppliers.

Although Adolph Sutro never wrote down his grand design, in newspaper interviews, he described his vision for a glass roof over the pools, and separate bathhouse and administration buildings; he did, however, remain vague on specifics. He'd leave those details to some future date and a yet-to-be selected architect. In the meantime, Sutro used his engineering skills to design the system of waterways, settling ponds, and concrete swimming tanks.

On August 5, 1891, Adolph Sutro placed a notice in the San Francisco papers, announcing a design competition for his new Baths:

> To Architects. The undersigned invites Architects to furnish designs for structures at his proposed bathing establishment, consisting of arrangements of bathhouses and offices:

(OPPOSITE) CONSTRUCTION IN PROGRESS: 1891 (TOP) AND 1893 (BOTTOM). NOTE THAT WORK HAS NOT YET STARTED ON THE IRON COLUMNS THAT WOULD SUPPORT THE VAST ROOF.

T H E   P O N D   B E C O M E S   T H E   B A T H S .

also for glass to cover baths. Premium for best approved design, $500, designs to be submitted on or before August 31, 1891. For particulars inquire of F. T. Newberry at his office, room 30, Montgomery Block.

—Adolph Sutro[11]

Immediately following the announcement of the design competition, which gave interested architects less than a month to respond, the *Chronicle* ran a story titled "Baths at the Beach. Adolph Sutro Building a Big Resort." In the article, Sutro shared his visions for the structures and grounds that would eventually materialize. There would be two large buildings for bathtubs, Turkish baths, restaurants, and clubrooms, he said, and another for offices. The concrete seawall nearing completion on the west side of the main tank would be topped by dressing rooms with a bandstand built above them. Terraces with seats for spectators would be built on east side of the cove overlooking the tanks.

Sutro continued: "Covering the whole space, terraces, seawall, tanks, esplanade and all, will be a great roof built of iron and glass in the central part and tailing off into wood or metal over the seats." Within the swimming tanks would be slides, diving boards, trapezes, and "one or two large fountains."

Sutro also had plans to utilize solar power to heat his Baths: "It is calculated that the water in the main tank will be raised from 10 to 15 degrees above the average ocean temperature by exposure to the sun in enclosed spaces and without artificial heat."

Sutro told the reporter he had already spent $100,000 on the Baths, and would probably spend another $200,000 before he was done, but didn't intend to keep the building when it was finished: "At first I will run the place myself, but when its success is assured and everything is in perfect working order I will probably lease the whole place."[12]

Impatient as always, Sutro didn't wait for the winning architectural

A medieval-looking sluice gate released seawater from the Point Lobos catch basin into the canal leading to the Baths.

THE WINNING PROPOSAL BY ARCHITECTS LEMME AND COLLEY,
NOVEMBER 1891.

firm to be announced before he began implementing another portion of the plan he had out-lined to the reporter. In September 1891, he started soliciting bids for the first building at the baths, a "Proposed Heating & Power Plant" to be built adjacent to the aquarium. The new structure would house boilers to heat water for generating electrical power and a laundry for the daily washing of hundreds of suits and towels.

Someone must have convinced Sutro that sunlight alone wouldn't be an effective means of heating the expansive pools; early drawings included alternatives for routing exhaust steam from the boilers into pipes beneath the tanks to heat the water. (The latter feature was never constructed.)[13]

The awarding of the architectural contract for the Baths took place on November 11, 1891, when the San Francisco firm of Emil S. Lemme and C. J. Colley was announced as the win-ner of the design competition. The sketch map of their winning proposal, published in the *Chronicle,* showed a steel-and-glass roof covering the baths and bleachers, just as Sutro had described, but with other touches that won the firm the contract. Instead of placing dressing rooms on the ocean side of the tanks, thus obstructing the view, Lemme and Colley's design set the dressing rooms beneath the bleachers on the south and east sides of the cove, leaving an uninterrupted vista of the Pacific through a wall of glass windows. A separate Queen Anne-style building to the east of the swimming tanks was designed "for Hammam [Turkish] baths, clubrooms, restaurants and café."

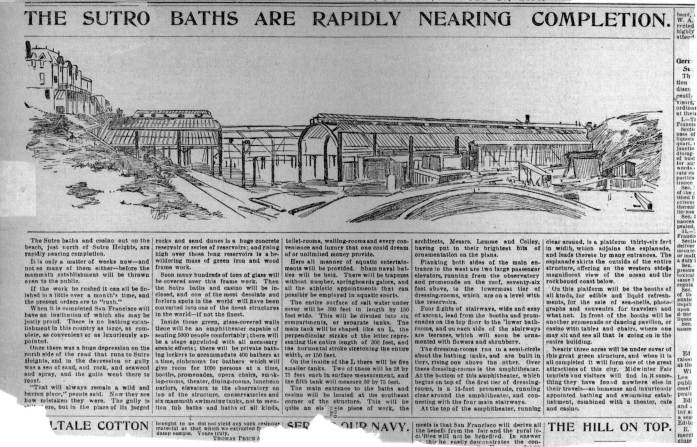

THE MORNING CALL, SAN FRANCISCO, SUNDAY, AUGUST 27, 1893.

THE SUTRO BATHS ARE RAPIDLY NEARING COMPLETION.

The Sutro baths and casino out on the beach, just north of Sutro Heights, are rapidly nearing completion.

It is only a matter of weeks now—and not so many of them either—before the mammoth establishment will be thrown open to the public.

If the work be rushed it can all be finished in a little over a month's time, and the present orders are to "rush."

When it is completed San Francisco will have an institution of which she may be justly proud. There is no bathing establishment in this country as large, as complete, as convenient or as luxuriously appointed.

Once there was a huge depression on the north side of the road that runs to Sutro Heights, and in the depression or gully was a sea of sand, and rock, and seaweed and spray, and the gulls went there to roost.

"That will always remain a wild and barren place," people said. Now they see how mistaken they were. The gully is ... ere, but in the place of its jagged

rocks and sand dunes is a huge concrete reservoir or series of reservoirs; and rising high over these long reservoirs is a bewildering mass of green iron and wood frame work.

Soon many hundreds of tons of glass will be covered over this frame work. Then the Sutro baths and casino will be inclosed, and one of the most desolate and forlorn spots in the world will have been converted into one of the finest structures in the world—if not the finest.

Inside these green, glass-covered walls there will be an amphitheater capable of seating 5000 people comfortably; there will be a stage appointed with all necessary scenic effects; there will be private bathing lockers to accommodate 400 bathers at a time, clubrooms for bathers which will give room for 1000 persons at a time, booths, promenades, opera chairs, smoking-rooms, theater, dining-rooms, luncheon parlors, elevators to the observatory on top of the structure, conservatories and six mammoth swimming tanks, not to mention tub baths and baths of all kinds,

toilet-rooms, waiting-rooms and every convenience and luxury that one could dream of or unlimited money provide.

Here all manner of aquatic entertainments will be provided. Sham naval battles will be held. There will be trapezes without number, springboards galore, and all the athletic appointments that can possibly be employed in aquatic sports.

The entire surface of salt water under cover will be 300 feet in length by 150 feet wide. This will be divided into six compartments, or separate tanks. The main tank will be shaped like an L. The perpendicular stroke of the letter representing the entire length of 300 feet, and the horizontal stroke stretching the entire width, or 150 feet.

On the inside of the L there will be five smaller tanks. Two of these will be 28 by 75 feet each in surface measurement, and the fifth tank will measure 50 by 75 feet.

The main entrance to the baths and casino will be located at the southeast corner of the structure. This will be quite an ela... te piece of work, the

architects, Messrs. Lemme and Colley, having put in their brightest bits of ornamentation on the plans.

Flanking both sides of the main entrance to the west are two large passenger elevators, running from the observatory and promenade on the roof, seventy-six feet above, to the lowermost tier of dressing-rooms, which are on a level with the reservoirs.

Four flights of stairways, wide and easy of ascent, lead from the booths and promenades on the top floor to the lower bathrooms, and on each side of the stairways are terraces, which will soon be ornamented with flowers and shrubbery.

The dressing-rooms run in a semi-circle about the bathing tanks, and are built in tiers, rising one above the other. Over these dressing-rooms is the amphitheater. At the bottom of this amphitheater, which begins on top of the first tier of dressing-rooms, is a 14-foot promenade, running clear around the amphitheater, and connecting with the four main stairways.

At the top of the amphitheater, running

clear around, is a platform thirty-six feet in width, which adjoins the esplanade, and leads thereto by many entrances. The esplanade skirts the outside of the entire structure, offering on the western side a magnificent view of the ocean and the rockbound coast below.

On this platform will be the booths of all kinds, for edible and liquid refreshments, for the sale of sea-shells, photographs and souvenirs for travelers and what not. In front of the booths will be another promenade or dancing pavilion, or casino with tables and chairs, where one may sit and see all that is going on in the entire building.

Nearly three acres will be under cover of this great green structure, and when it is all completed it will form one of the great attractions of this city. Midwinter Fair tourists and visitors will find in it something they have found nowhere else in their travels—an immense and luxuriously appointed bathing and swimming establishment, combined with a theater, cafe and casino.

A STORY IN THE AUGUST 27, 1893, *SAN FRANCISCO MORNING CALL* WAS OVERLY OPTIMISTIC.
OPENING DAY AT THE BATHS WAS STILL MORE THAN 15 MONTHS AWAY.

A series of converging arched trusses would cover the pools, while a smaller span would protect the bleachers to the east. Twin elevators in towers would carry patrons from the bathhouse level to the swimming tanks 50 feet below.

The dimensions for the buildings were impressive.

The main swimming pavilion, with its pools, covered bleachers, and dressing rooms, would be 360 feet by 268 feet, and the turreted bathhouse/restaurant to the east would be 104 feet by 84 feet.

The architects also managed to incorporate Sutro's existing swimming tanks, powerhouse, and water supply system with only a few changes. (They had little choice, since this infrastructure was already in place.) The *Chronicle* story included a description of how these water works as designed by Sutro originally functioned:

> The salt seawater is to be led in from a large settling basin on the north of the main building. From this basin the water will pour into a channel with concrete walls and bottom ten feet wide and one foot below high-water level. Sluice gates at different intervals along this channel, which is to run the whole length of the building, will enable the supply of water to be controlled, while a main sluice gate between the settling pond and channel will be a means of cutting off the supply entirely and so draining the baths when necessary. [14]

Sutro must have been a difficult client. Since he had already begun constructing portions of the Baths before he had even chosen his architects, Lemme and Colley were presented with an immense foundation (in the form of the swimming tanks) complete with an elaborate plumbing system and, now, a steam power plant.

ADOLPH SUTRO SPORTED MUTTON-CHOP SIDEBURNS PARTLY TO CONCEAL A KNIFE SCAR ACQUIRED DURING HIS YOUTH.

THREE
Building the Baths

ONE OF LEMME AND COLLEY'S first tasks was to get bids for putting a roof over the swimming tanks. Before long, they were collecting quotes from various steel and iron firms. However, finding a supplier and writing the contract took nearly a year. As bids were being solicited, A. D. Ottewell was brought on board as supervising engineer for the planned ironwork. A. O. Harrison, who had been Sutro's foreman during construction of the aquarium and swimming pond, became supervisor of the continuing masonry work. G. W. Hansbrough rounded out Sutro's team; he was in charge of carpentry (i.e., non-ironwork) construction of the bathhouse and boiler house.[15]

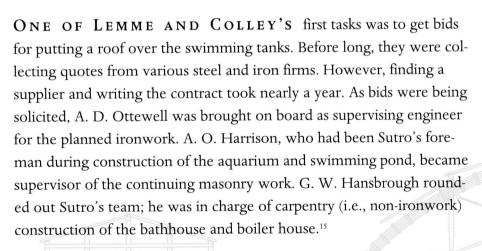

(ABOVE) GLAZIERS INSTALLED MORE THAN TWO ACRES OF GLASS OVER THE SWIMMING TANKS.
(OPPOSITE) CARPENTERS ASSEMBLED THE ARCHED WOODEN TRUSSES THAT WOULD SPAN THE BATHS.

THE MANSARD-ROOFED BOILER HOUSE BEGAN AS A FREE-STANDING BUILDING. IT WAS SHORTLY ENGULFED BY THE BATHS STRUCTURE GROWING BEHIND IT.

A RARE INTERIOR VIEW OF THE LAUNDRY. THE INTIMIDATING CONTRAPTION AT RIGHT IS A MANGLE, WHICH WAS USED TO PRESS AND FLATTEN TOWELS.

The first structure completed was the Baths' powerhouse and laundry building. The *Morning Call* reported on its construction during the summer of 1892. The story revealed that in August, the building had reached the height of the third floor and had boilers and dynamos on its first floor, laundry equipment and dryers on the second, and employee living quarters on the third. An 84-foot tower would complete the building, which would connect to a roadway on the east side via a bridge. The newspaper article went on to describe Adolph Sutro's comprehensive plan, which included park grounds surrounding the yet-to-be-built bathhouse and office.[16]

In October 1892, one of Sutro's on-site representatives, W. C. Little, visited the Baths and reported back to his boss on the progress he'd observed. Little wrote at length about the various terraces and drainage systems being installed on the hillside east of the tanks, and noted that the pools themselves were in the process of being painted. (He estimated it would take three coats.)

Little also reported to Sutro on the condition of the power plant: "Boiler and Laundry House. Men putting up balustrade around the roof and working on upper rear veranda."[17] A photograph of the Baths taken from Fisherman's Rock (aka Flagstaff Rock) at this time matches Little's description nearly exactly, even showing the workers in the process of installing a railing along the parapet of the boiler house. To its right, a forest of timbers marks the location of the east bleachers under construction.

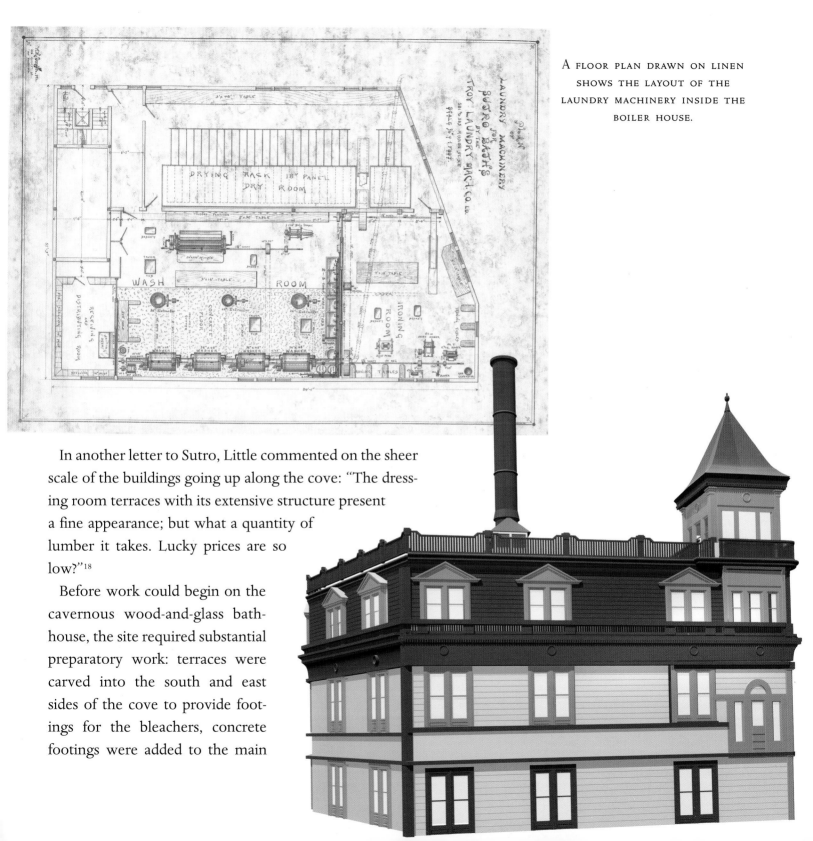

In another letter to Sutro, Little commented on the sheer scale of the buildings going up along the cove: "The dressing room terraces with its extensive structure present a fine appearance; but what a quantity of lumber it takes. Lucky prices are so low?"[18]

Before work could begin on the cavernous wood-and-glass bathhouse, the site required substantial preparatory work: terraces were carved into the south and east sides of the cove to provide footings for the bleachers, concrete footings were added to the main

A SERIES OF CONSTRUCTION PHOTOS TAKEN IN 1893-1894, FROM THE COLLECTION OF THE CALIFORNIA HISTORICAL SOCIETY.

SUTRO'S GLASS PALACE

tank to support the iron roof columns, roads to the site were improved and graded, and two large reservoirs were excavated east of the structure to hold spring water for the boilers and a projected freshwater plunge tank.

In September 1892, the *Examiner* reported on the progress:

> There are buildings to be put up, and an immense amount of grading to be done, and the fittings of the whole establishment to be provided.
>
> There is only one of the buildings yet under way, and that is the engine house and laundry. This is nearly complete. . . . This week the building to contain the dressing rooms will be commenced, as soon as the grading is done. This structure will be on the slope of the hill that leads up from the swimming tanks to the fresh water reservoir. There are to be upwards of 500 rooms.

However, major elements of Lemme and Colley's grand design were already being eliminated: "The building for tub baths, with apartments for the Turkish, Russian and other bathing processes, will be deferred until all the others are done. Its location will be just at the north of the fresh water reservoir and on the same level with the upper tier of dressing rooms." As it turned out, the separate bathhouse was never constructed.

The story concluded with another revelation about Sutro's continually evolving vision for the area: "It is Mr. Sutro's intention to eventually erect a hotel on the bluff of Parallel Point, to the north of the bathing place and between the Cliff House and Point Lobos."[19]

About the same time, Harrison's quarry crews constructed a rock-and-concrete staircase descending from the flattened tip of Point Lobos to the level of the water channel leading to the former aquarium. Observation platforms along the staircase allowed visitors to watch waves crashing into the catch basin; a large sluice gate at the foot of this staircase could stop or constrain the flow of water from the basin. The high quality of workmanship on the staircase indicates it was probably intended to be

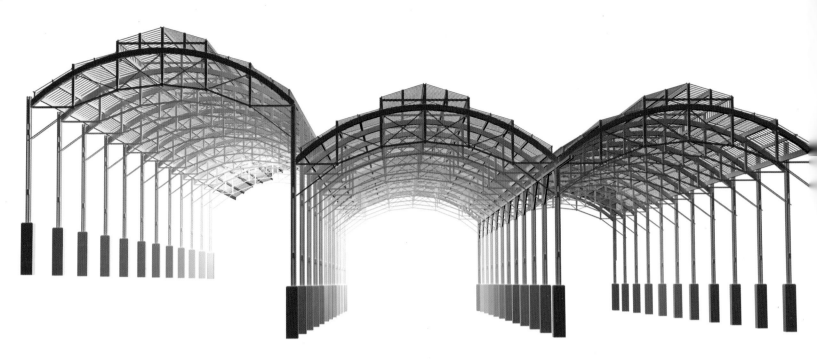

part of one of Sutro's never-finished developments atop the point, such as his coastal promenade or luxury hotel.

As late as fall 1892, Sutro and his architects were still considering different designs for separate bathhouse and administrative buildings on the flat area east of the tanks. At some point, Lemme and Colley revised their original plans and proposed a single, sprawling structure that would enclose all the functions Sutro envisioned. In its final form, Sutro Baths would incorporate swimming pools, bleachers, changing rooms, promenade, powerhouse, office areas, restaurants, clubrooms, and museum exhibits into one massive building measuring more than two acres in area.

The final design for the glass roofs over the pools—perhaps the most iconic characteristic of Sutro Baths—was actually one of the last features settled upon. As originally designed by Lemme and Colley, a single arched roof measuring 150 feet across would have spanned all the pools, while a smaller cantilevered roof to the east covered the bleacher seats. Perhaps for ease of construction, or as a cost-cutting measure, the architects now proposed two smaller roofs over the pools. When construction began, the final design featured three arched glass roofs of nearly equal proportions: two spanning the pools and a third over the seating and promenade areas.

ADOLPH SUTRO INSPECTING HIS GREAT WORK IN PROGRESS. THE ORIGINAL BOILER HOUSE IS IN THE BACKGROUND.

EVOLUTION FROM AN OPEN-AIR BATHING STATION TO THE COMPLETED SUTRO BATHS.

This design change in the roof necessitated adding an additional line of iron support columns along the centerline of the Baths. As a result, Lemme and Colley incorporated ten vertical columns along the pools' edges, including three on concrete pylons rising from the middle of the main tank.

Throughout the spring and summer of 1893, ironworkers erected the towering iron support columns while carpenters assembled and raised the wooden trusses that would support the three roofs with their thousands of glass panes. On July 28, 1893, construction superintendent Hansbrough reported to Sutro, "The work at Baths is now going ahead first rate. All the Trusses, Purlines, & Ridge Trusses are now in position." In effect, the framework of the Baths was complete. From that date forward, construction

ADOLPH SUTRO RELAXING IN THE LIBRARY OF HIS SUTRO HEIGHTS HOME.

focused on carpentry work; plumbing; installing electrical systems; putting up acres of glass; and the seemingly endless task of painting all the woodwork, steel, and concrete throughout the cavernous structure.[20]

Sutro felt his Baths would be ready for public use in spring 1894, and announced his plans for a grand dedication on April 29, his sixty-fourth birthday. He gave a tour of the building to a reporter from the *San Francisco Evening Bulletin* and provided his own perspective on the background and design of the structure.

Sutro, whom no one would've described as humble, told the reporter he had been so inspired by the location that he became determined to outdo the baths of classical Rome:

> A small place would not satisfy me. I must have it large, pretentious, in keeping with the Heights and the great ocean itself, so I filled the whole cove and gave my building a frontage of 350 feet, which, if I am not mistaken, is the largest extent ever given to a similar structure. The largest of the Roman baths was said to have only 200 feet front and considerable less surface area. The interior had to be in keeping. Nothing short of an amphitheatre seemed to answer. That I did not quite copy, but the impression made on the mind by the design I have followed is very much the same. The vastness is all there—the great open room—and the circus [i.e., the tanks and bathers], as it were, far below. . . .

As for the natural world of the former Seal Rock Beach that had been destroyed by construction of the Baths, Sutro was dismissive. "The useless exemplar of geological erosion has become the home of one of humanities [sic] greatest works."

The reporter also documented Sutro's tight rein during construction. "It was found that Mr. Sutro had been his own architect and contractor and foreman throughout. Mr. Hansbrough and Mr. Harrison were merely his lieutenants. They conferred with him on every matter of detail. Messrs. Colley and Lemme were the architects, but the great design, the 'tout ensemble,' was the creation of Mr. Sutro's brain alone."

In a revealing exchange, the reporter asked Sutro how much the structure had cost. "Too much," muttered Mr. Sutro in an aside, then turned and responded in a louder and more boisterous voice: "It cost over half a million dollars."[21]

THE SOUTH END OF THE MAIN TANK INCORPORATED THE NATURAL ROCK CLIFFS OF THE FORMER COVE.

Construction on the Baths was nearly complete, but the grand opening kept being pushed back. Only a few days before the planned April 29 event, a dreadful accident occurred. A newspaper headline blared: "A Fearful Fall at Sutro's Baths. A Scaffolding Gives Way & Two Workmen Are Crushed on the Stone Floor." The story explained that the two laborers had been working on the trusses 50 feet above the tanks when their temporary scaffold collapsed and they fell into one of the empty pools below.[22] These were the first recorded deaths at Sutro Baths.

Work was still in progress at the time of the accident, and while it's not recorded if the workers' deaths were the reason the opening was postponed, another delay shortly arose. But this time, it was political.

On May 1, 1894, Sutro announced that the Baths would not be opened because of a growing feud with Southern Pacific Railroad over what he considered exorbitant fares being charged for its trains to the Cliff House. When Sutro had helped build the Ferries & Cliff House Railroad in the

A SMALL PLACE WOULD NOT SATISFY ME. I MUST HAVE IT
LARGE, PRETENTIOUS, IN KEEPING WITH THE HEIGHTS AND
THE GREAT OCEAN ITSELF.
                                            —ADOLPH SUTRO

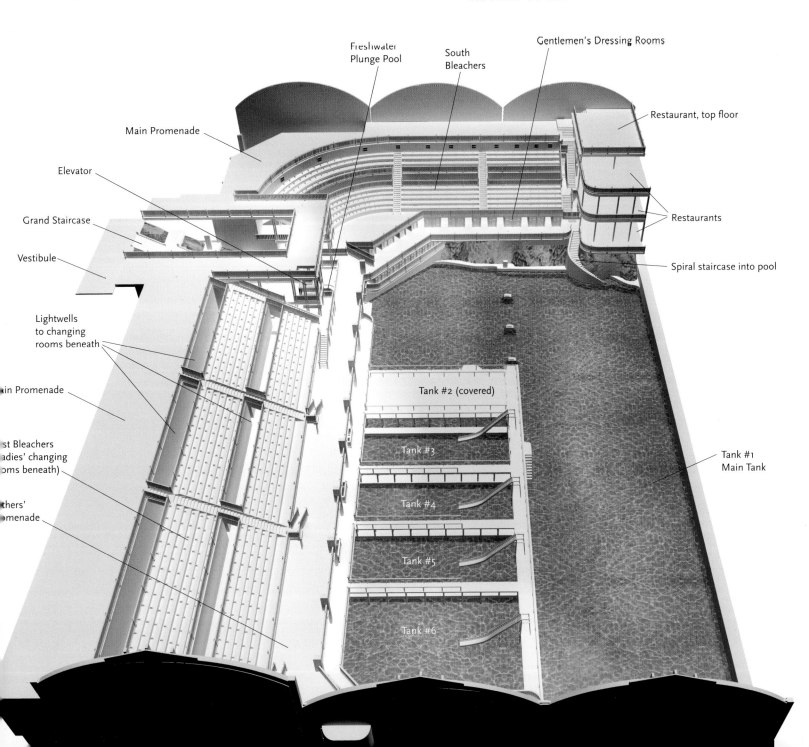

Freshwater
Plunge Pool

South
Bleachers

Gentlemen's Dressing Rooms

Restaurant, top floor

Main Promenade

Elevator

Grand Staircase

Vestibule

Restaurants

Spiral staircase into pool

Lightwells
to changing
rooms beneath

in Promenade

st Bleachers
adies' changing
oms beneath)

thers'
menade

Tank #2 (covered)

Tank #3

Tank #4

Tank #5

Tank #6

Tank #1
Main Tank

Photograph by W. C. Billington

1880s, he insisted that transfers be offered so that the fare to the Cliff was no more than 5 cents. When Southern Pacific (SP) purchased the miniscule railroad in 1892, they eliminated the transfer policy and effectively doubled the fare. The war was on.

Sutro announced that his Baths would remain closed until the 5-cent fare was reinstated. "I now find myself ready to open the baths. . . . But I will not open these baths without some assurances that I can have cheap fares, good facilities and trains till 12 o'clock."

Sutro meant business; he erected fences around Sutro Heights and the Cliff House and began charging a 25-cent admission to anyone arriving on the Ferries & Cliff House trains. (This was no small matter; a quarter in 1894 equaled about $5.50 in today's buying power.) Sutro also announced that he was prepared to delay the grand opening of the Baths for as long as five years to make his point.[23]

The fact that Sutro was running for mayor of San Francisco at the time also factored into his battle with Southern Pacific. Sutro was a Populist, and the SP was a widely despised monopoly, so taking on the railroad in a head-to-head battle over reduced fares while holding the Baths' grand opening for ransom would, he hoped, gain him votes. And it worked. Before the fall elections, SP relented and reinstated the transfer policy. It was too late. In November 1894, Sutro was

THE LADIES OF THE NATIONAL MEDICAL CONVENTION GOT A PREVIEW OF THE NEARLY FINISHED BATHS ON JUNE 8, 1894. ADOLPH SUTRO IS IN THE FIRST ROW AT LEFT.

elected mayor of San Francisco.

Eventually, "officially" opening the Baths to the public became something of a technical point. Sutro insisted that as long as patrons weren't allowed to swim, the Baths weren't open. However, beginning in May 1894 and going on for nearly two years, he allowed visitors to explore the promenades and exhibits and even offered public concerts, professional swimming competitions, exhibitions of trick diving, and other aquatic entertainments—just not public bathing.[24]

Sutro stubbornly held to this tactic until March 1896, when, at long last, a grand dedication was held and the public was allowed into the pools. This period of quasi-operation has given rise to two "birthdays" for the Sutro Baths: May 1894, when the public was first admitted into the structure, and March 1896, when an official dedication took place and the tanks were opened to swimmers.

A Sutro Railroad streetcar, circa 1896. This clean, quiet technology had been introduced to America only a few years before. Sutro's chateau-inspired Cliff House towers in the background.

SUTRO'S GLASS PALACE

DURING THE TWENTY-TWO MONTHS the formal opening was on hold, Sutro busied himself with other projects that would have direct impact on the Baths: acquiring artworks and stuffed animals from the defunct Woodward's Gardens in the Mission District, purchasing leftover exhibits and rides from the 1894 Midwinter Exposition in Golden Gate Park, building a new and more grandiose Cliff House, and constructing an electric streetcar line.

The Midwinter Exposition, a scaled-down version of Chicago's Columbian Exposition of 1893, took place from January to June 1894, and included many of the exhibits and sideshow attractions transported from the original Chicago site. When the Midwinter fair closed, Sutro picked up exhibits and fair fixtures at bargain-basement rates. In addition to benches, statuary, and concession kiosks, Sutro purchased several rides and attractions and moved them from the park to a plateau overlooking the Baths (today known as Merrie Way). There, along a central midway, Sutro re-erected several of the most popular attractions and christened the collection the "Sutro Pleasure Grounds." These included a mirror maze, a scenic-railway roller coaster, and the 100-foot-diameter Firth Wheel, a half-sized version of the original Ferris wheel that had been a hit at the Chicago exposition.[25]

Sutro's other project was the Sutro Railroad, an electric streetcar line established specifically to challenge SP's train monopoly to the Cliff House. His new line ran out Clement Street for much of its route, made a few jogs, and terminated in a new depot on Cliff Avenue. From the depot, a covered walkway led right into the Baths. Best of all, the Sutro Railroad offered passengers free transfers and an assured 5-cent fare. On October 26, 1894, Adolph Sutro announced that work had begun on his new line.[26]

The Sutro Railroad began operation on February 1, 1896, which, by a carefully contrived coincidence, just happened to be the same date that Sutro's "new" Cliff House was also dedicated. Sutro announced that, at long last, the Baths would also open to the public. The new target date was set for March 14, 1896.

FOUR
The Baths Open

AS THE 1896 GRAND OPENING APPROACHED, Sutro's workers put
finishing touches on the building, swimming tanks, and utility systems. A new general
manager was hired, Colonel T. P. Robinson, whose job it would be to oversee all the
Baths amusements, including the growing midway. The night before the grand opening, a complete dress rehearsal of the mechanical systems took place. The *Call*
reported that there were 58 arc lamps and 1,600 incandescent bulbs in the structure,
and that all worked perfectly. Seawater, heated by the powerhouse boilers, moved
continuously from the powerhouse through the feed canal and into the tanks. As
planned, the six saltwater tanks were each warmed to varying temperatures. In the
large tank, the temperature was between 78 and 80 degrees. The coldest tank, according to the news story, was the freshwater plunge, at 62 degrees.[27]

After the repeated delays, it was somewhat depressing that only 7,000 people (less
than a third of the building's capacity) attended the events on March 14. The low
turnout was probably due to the stormy weather that pummeled the city that day, but,
as the newspapers pointed out, the entire event was rather anticlimactic. Sutro's had
been open to the public since May 1894 for visitation and special events, and the only
really new feature, aside from thunderous dedicatory speeches, was the opportunity
to finally swim in the pools. And a blustery winter day at the seaside was not con-
ducive to attracting crowds of swimmers.[28]

A VIEW LOOKING UP THE MAIN ENTRANCE STAIRCASE TOWARD THE DOORS LEADING TO CLIFF
AVENUE (LATER POINT LOBOS AVENUE).

How the Baths Worked

The November 1894 edition of the magazine *Pacific Electrician* contained a lengthy story on Sutro Baths, including a detailed description of its mechanical systems, especially how the boiler plant and electrical systems operated. This story gives us the first glimpse of how the Baths actually functioned.

Seawater from waves trapped in the catch basin first made its way to the settling pond, where sand and seaweed were allowed to settle to the bottom. The clarified seawater was then pumped to the adjacent powerhouse through suction intake pipes. Inside the power plant, the cold water was pumped through a coil of steel pipes running through a condenser box.

Exhaust steam coming out of the powerhouse engines was directed into the condenser box. When the hot steam hit the cold seawater pipes, it condensed into fresh water, which was pumped back into the boilers. This process simultaneously transferred heat from the steam to the seawater running through the condenser pipes.

The warmed seawater coming out of the condenser box was directed into a network of small canals leading to the swimming tanks. The temperatures in the individual tanks was adjusted by simply opening and closing sluice gates at various points to mix hot condenser water with unheated water coming directly from the settling pond.

The *Pacific Electrician* noted that the underpowered boiler system dated to 1892 and couldn't raise the temperature sufficiently to heat all the tanks, but that a solution was at hand, since the powerhouse was

THE ORIGINAL BOILER HOUSE CONTAINED AN UNDERPOWERED STEAM ENGINE AND DYNAMO FOR GENERATING ELECTRICITY.

IN 1895, AN ADDITION WAS CONSTRUCTED FOR THE IMMENSE STEAM ENGINES THAT PRODUCED ELECTRICITY FOR THE SUTRO RAILROAD. THEY PROVIDED AMPLE POWER FOR BOTH THE STREETCAR LINE AND THE BATHS.

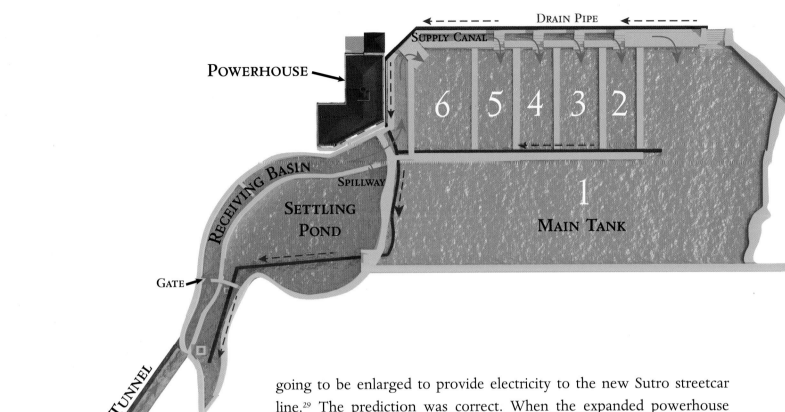

DRAIN PIPE

SUPPLY CANAL

POWERHOUSE

6 5 4 3 2

RECEIVING BASIN

SPILLWAY

SETTLING POND

1

MAIN TANK

GATE

TUNNEL

CATCH BASIN

OCEAN WAVES

going to be enlarged to provide electricity to the new Sutro streetcar line.[29] The prediction was correct. When the expanded powerhouse went into operation in early 1896, condenser water from a total of five boilers was able to heat the six saltwater pools to an average temperature of 70 degrees Fahrenheit.[30]

A tradition soon developed of heating different pools to varying temperatures, ranging from natural ocean temperature (50 to 55 degrees) up to as warm as 90 degrees. The fresh-water plunge was maintained at the temperature at which the water emerged from the nearby hillside spring: very, very cold.

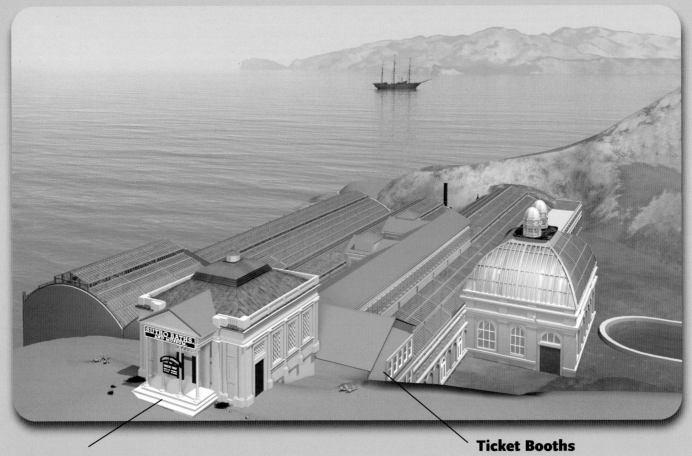

Pedestrian Entrance

Ticket Booths

IT WAS A LONG WAY FROM THE MAIN ENTRANCE on Cliff Avenue down to the actual swimming pools, nearly 100 feet below. Visitors came in through a **pedestrian entrance** designed as a Greek temple, which was actually the top landing of a staircase that descended from street level to the ticket booths and museum level.

Visitors pose for group portraits at the entrance to the Greek Temple and its famous redwood tree cross-section.

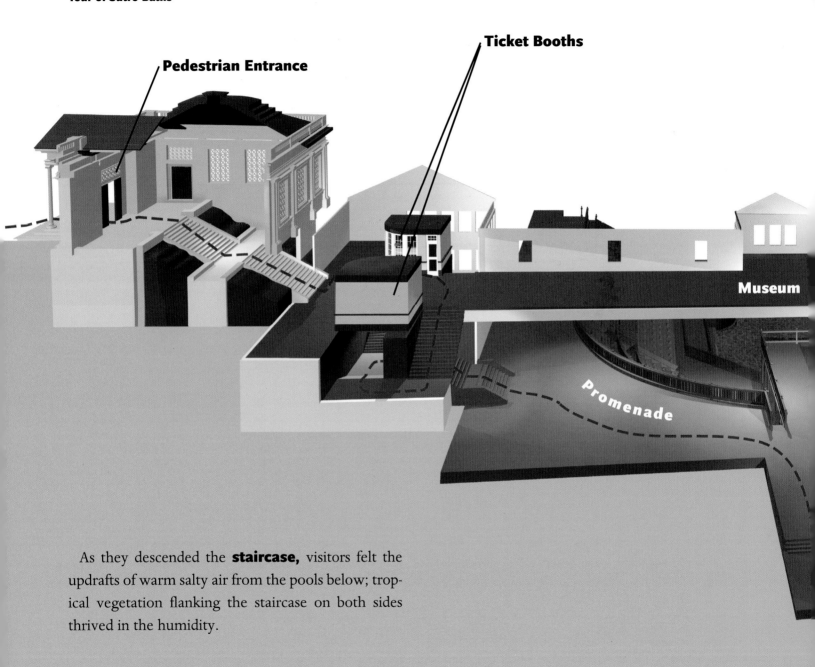

Pedestrian Entrance

Ticket Booths

Museum

Promenade

As they descended the **staircase,** visitors felt the updrafts of warm salty air from the pools below; tropical vegetation flanking the staircase on both sides thrived in the humidity.

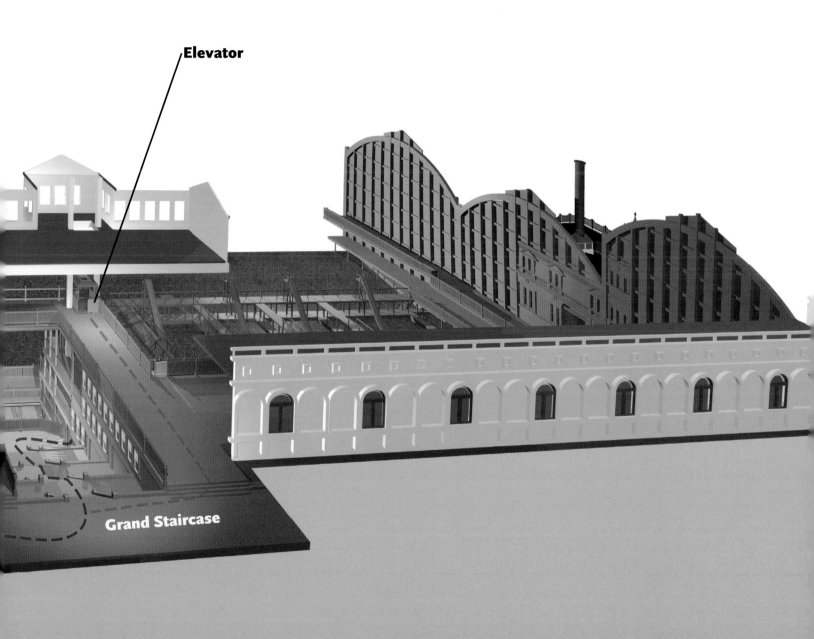

Elevator

Grand Staircase

At the **ticket booths**, visitors paid 10 cents for general admission, and an additional 15 cents for admission to the pools, which included a swimsuit, towel, and a private changing room.

Grand Staircase

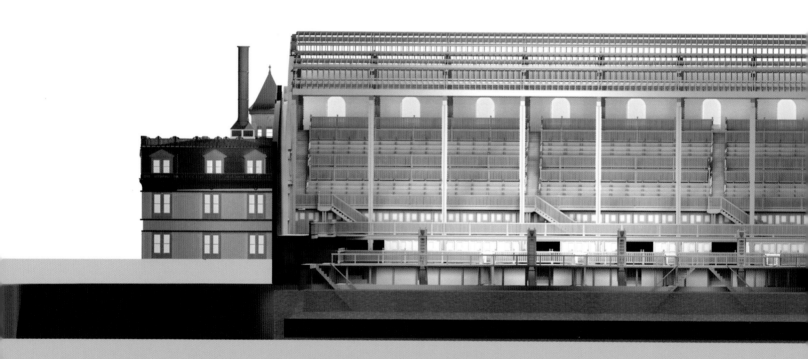

A cross-section through the Baths. The elevation change from the street level entrance (upper right) to the pools was nearly 100 feet.

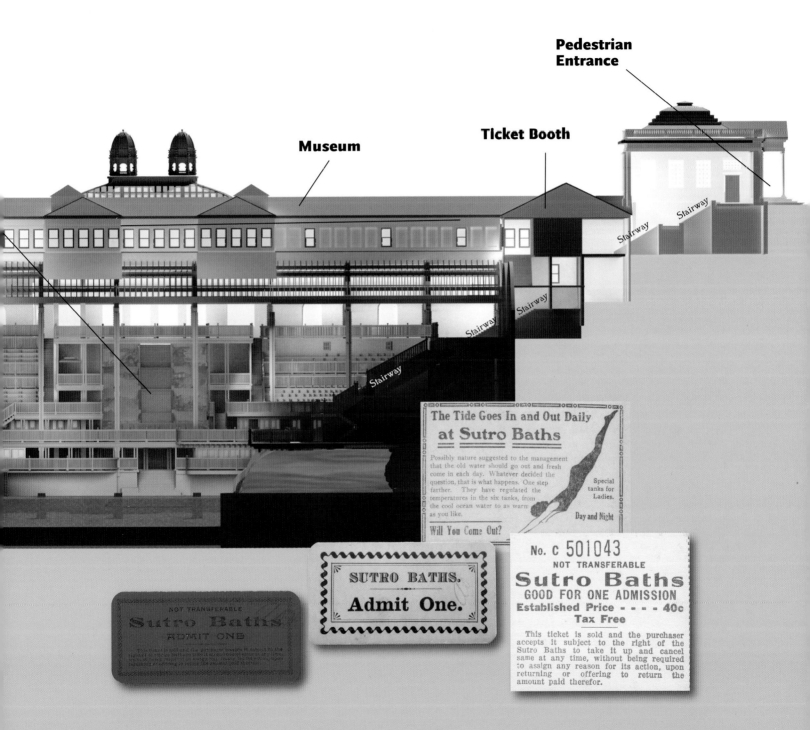

Pedestrian Entrance

Museum

Ticket Booth

Stairway

Stairway

Stairway

Stairway

Stairway

The Tide Goes In and Out Daily at Sutro Baths

Possibly nature suggested to the management that the old water should go out and fresh come in each day. Whatever decided the question, that is what happens. One step farther. They have regulated the temperatures in the six tanks, from the cool ocean water to as warm as you like.

Special tanks for Ladies.

Day and Night

Will You Come Out?

SUTRO BATHS.
Admit One.

NOT TRANSFERABLE
Sutro Baths
ADMIT ONE

This ticket is sold and the purchaser accepts it subject to the right of the Sutro Baths to take it up and cancel same at any time, without being required to assign any reason for its action, upon returning or offering to return the amount paid therefor.

No. C 501043
NOT TRANSFERABLE
Sutro Baths
GOOD FOR ONE ADMISSION
Established Price - - - - 40c
Tax Free

This ticket is sold and the purchaser accepts it subject to the right of the Sutro Baths to take it up and cancel same at any time, without being required to assign any reason for its action, upon returning or offering to return the amount paid therefor.

The ticket level housed Sutro's **museum,** a quirky mélange of curiosities that Sutro had collected during his world travels. Here, directly behind the ticket stiles, visitors were greeted by the immense stuffed sea lion named Ben Butler who had once reigned over Seal Rocks. Behind Ben were cases holding Egyptian mummies; snowshoes; stuffed polar bears, pythons, and birds; and display cases filled with endless seashells and geology specimens. This level also served as the upper terminus for an elevator that descended to the pool level.

THE EGYPTIAN MUMMIES AND SARCOPHAGI WERE AMONG THE MOST POPULAR DISPLAYS IN THE MUSEUM.

BEN BUTLER ON DISPLAY AT THE ENTRANCE TO THE MUSEUM.

A DISPLAY CASE CRAMMED WITH TAXIDERMY SPECIMENS ON THE PROMENADE LEVEL.

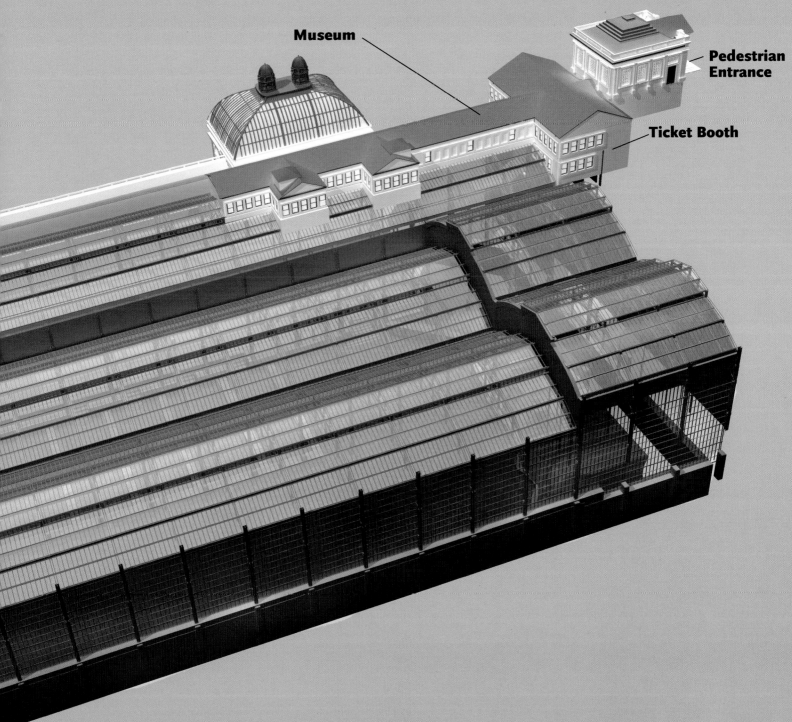

Museum

Pedestrian Entrance

Ticket Booth

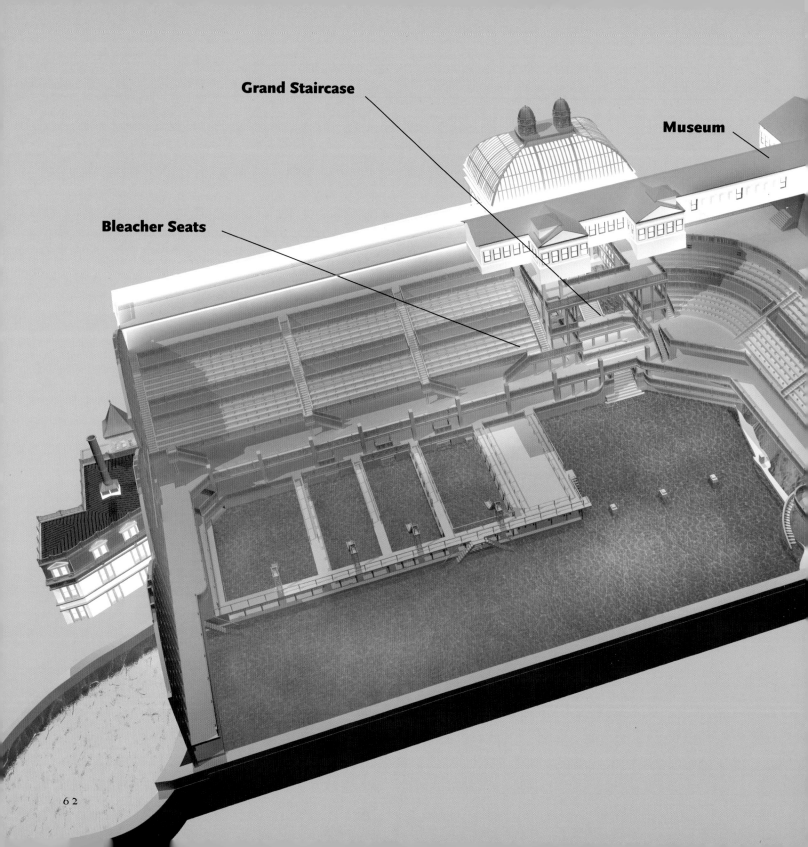

Grand Staircase

Museum

Bleacher Seats

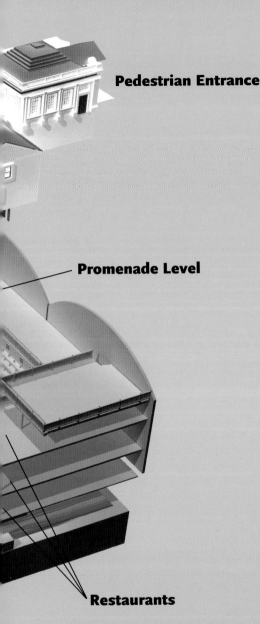

Pedestrian Entrance

Promenade Level

Restaurants

THE PROMENADE LEVEL WITH MORE POTTED PALMS. THE LARGE WHITE PAVILION AT RIGHT WAS A SODA FOUNTAIN.

From the museum level, twin staircases descended another story and emerged on the **promenade level.** This J-shaped terrace ran the length of the south and east sides of the building, overlooking the swimming tanks located 50 feet below. It also held the checkroom, where patrons headed for the pools exchanged tickets for swimsuits and towels before descending to the locker rooms below. Non-swimmers could entertain themselves exploring the exhibit rooms, food concessions, stereograph viewers, and yet more museum cases that lined the promenade.

THE GRAND STAIRCASE DESCENDED FROM THE
PROMENADE LEVEL TO THE SWIMMING TANKS. WINDOWS
ON BOTH SIDES PROVIDED LIGHT TO CHANGING ROOMS
BENEATH THE BLEACHERS.

POSITIVELY FOR BATHERS ONLY

THE VESTIBULE LEVEL OF THE GRAND STAIRCASE. THE LARGE OBELISK WITH EAGLE WAS ONE OF SUTRO'S PURCHASES FROM THE 1894 MIDWINTER FAIR IN GOLDEN GATE PARK.

Swimmers descended a **grand staircase** from the promenade to the locker rooms and pool level. A large glass atrium, capped by a domed roof with twin cupolas, soared over the top of the grand staircase. Sutro had originally planned the atrium as a porte-cochere entrance, where upper-crust visitors could exit their horse-drawn coaches, but it never served this purpose.

PLANTERS FLANKED THE STAIRCASE. VEGETATION THRIVED IN THE HUMID AIR OF THE BATHS.

Elevator

Locker Area

Bleachers

**Changing
Rooms**

Grand Staircase

Farther down the grand staircase, entrances to the **locker area** branched off to the left and right.

Nestled beneath the bleachers, the locker area contained 517 individual **changing rooms** as well as showers, toilets, and clubrooms for organized groups. Swimmers peeled off along these stairs, ladies to the right and "gents" to the left. Once inside the changing areas, an attendant led each bather to a closet-sized changing room and gave them a brass check token. The attendant locked the room while the bather was in the pools, and unlocked it upon being shown the token. (Bathers either wore their token on a string around their neck or tucked it into a tiny pocket sewn into each bathing suit.)

No. 1263
SUTRO BATHS
GOOD FOR
BATHING SUIT
PRESENT AT SUIT COUNTER

No. 1263
ADMISSION
TO
DRESSING ROOM
PRESENT TO ATTENDANT

A MAZE OF CLOSET-SIZED CHANGING
ROOMS, EACH EQUIPPED WITH A BENCH AND A COUPLE OF
WALL HOOKS, FILLED THE AREA BENEATH THE BLEACHERS.

67

Wooden bleacher seats, stair-stepping down toward the pools, provided seating for thousands of spectators.

The grand staircase continued downward, finally ending at a lower promenade called the **bathers' promenade**, just a few feet above the pools.

At the very foot of the staircase, separate from the saltwater tanks, was the oval-shaped freshwater **plunge.** Filled by natural hillside springs, it was notorious as the Baths' coldest pool.

THE GRAND STAIRCASE TERMINATED AT A BALCONY OVERLOOKING THE FRESHWATER PLUNGE.

SUTRO BATHS BY THE NUMBERS

Length of Baths: 499.5 feet

Width of Baths: 254.1 feet

Amount of glass used: 100,000 superficial ft.

Iron in roof columns: 600 tons

Lumber: 3,500,000 feet

Concrete: 270,000 cubic feet

Seating capacity, amphitheater: 3,700

Seating capacity, promenade: 3,700

Holding capacity: 25,000

Salt water tanks: 6

Capacity of tanks: 1,804,962 gallons

Freshwater plunge tank: 1

Toboggan slides in baths: 7

Swinging rings: 30

Spring boards: 1

Private dressing rooms: 517

Club rooms, capacity: 1,110

Time required to fill tank by waves: 1 hour

Time required to fill tank by pump: 5 hours

Source: *P.G.&E Magazine*, September 1912

Shortly after the Baths opened, tank #2 was covered over to serve as a stage and exercise area.

Swimmers on the starting line at the 1913 Pacific Coast Swimming Championships. The famous Duke Kahanamoku is fourth from left.

Tank #2 (covered)
Tank #3
Tank #4
Tank #5
Tank #6
Tank #1 Main Tank

Slightly below the bathers' promenade were the **six main swimming tanks.** The largest was the L-shaped main tank (tank #1), which ran the entire length of the western wall of the Baths. Tucked within the L were five smaller, rectangular tanks numbered two through six. Diving platforms and slides and gymnast rings lined the pools' perimeters. Tank six was the warmest, and technically, was reserved for women and children, although period photos show that this rule was rarely obeyed.

The Main Tank (right) originally stretched 275 feet along the length of the Baths.

ACTIVITIES AT SUTRO BATHS weren't limited to swimming or browsing the museum's displays. Live entertainment was provided nearly every weekend in the form of band concerts, trick diving exhibitions, acrobatic acts, May Day celebrations, and animal acts. To accommodate the performances, pool number two was covered over and turned into a large stage. Thousands of people gathered in the bleacher seats to watch the entertainments taking place far below.

In their classic book *San Francisciana: Photographs of Sutro Baths,* historians Marilyn Blaisdell and her son, Robert Blaisdell, recount the vaudevillian delights presented at the Baths:

> Entertaining the spectators in 1896 and 1897 was, among others, Charles Cavill, the world-champion swimmer from Australia, who not only swam in exhibitions of his prowess, but performed what was announced as "the Monte Carlo Drowning Act." Other performers included Professor Karl, "the marvelous Anthropic Amphibian

FRITZ SCHEEL'S ORCHESTRA PERFORMING IN 1894.

A May Day festival in 1897 featured three maypoles and drew a crowd of 9,000.

who eats, drinks, smokes, writes, and sleeps under water . . ."; Charmian, "Queen of the air, the greatest girl aerialist in the world," whose "leaps and dives into a net from the trapeze have never been accomplished by a woman"; Professor M. H. Gay and his wonderful dog Jack, ". . . the highest diving dog act in the world"; Zeda, "the boneless boy wonder"; . . . the "midget Sandows" in a "three-round boxing exhibition"; and Professor Baker, who "enters the water in his ordinary costume with a gunnysack in his hand. He disappears underneath the surface, and while underneath, he undresses (a most difficult trick) and reappears above the water in bathing attire. A prize will be offered to any bather who can find his clothes and the gunnysack."

Attractions included a "Monster May Day Festival . . . a beautiful queen, triple May poles, 1,000 children in grand march and the butterfly ballet," which, said Gelett Burgess in 1897, was attended by "9,000 people packed tier upon tier . . . up and up to the tiptop promenade." There were various contests: a Grand International Tug of War; a Walking Under Water Contest with a 50-pound dumbbell in each hand— "the man who walks farthest and brings his dumbbells above the water will receive $2.50"; Diving for Gold; and a 50-yard doughnut race, where "each swimmer must devour six doughnuts before starting."[31]

ONE OF THE FIVE SMALL SALTWATER TANKS CROWDED WITH MALE SWIMMERS.

SUTRO'S GLASS PALACE

FIVE
Operating the Baths

ONCE THE BATHS had been formally dedicated, construction foreman A. O. Harrison was upgraded to general manager, the facility's first. He supervised a staff numbering upward of twenty lifeguards, ticket-takers, locker-room attendants, engineers, and maintenance personnel.

There were problems from the start. Storm waves repeatedly damaged the stone breakwater and causeway to Fisherman's Rock, boilers burned coal at a dizzying rate, waves smashed glass windows, and the great expanse of glass overhead leaked in the rain. In fact, leaking water was endangering many museum exhibits, including the huge stuffed sea lion Ben Butler; it was recommended that tarps be put over the sea lion and other vulnerable exhibits during rainy weather.[32]

A YEAR AFTER THE BATHS officially opened, the new attraction became the focus of a test case for a then-new civil rights law passed by the California State Legislature. The Dibble Bill, which had gone into effect on April 29, 1897, declared that "no railways, hotels, restaurants, barber-shops, bathhouses, and other like institutions licensed to serve the public shall discriminate against any well behaved citizen, no matter what his color."

On July 4, 1897, John Harris came to Sutro Baths with a few white friends and bought a 25-cent ticket, which entitled him to general admission, a bathing suit, and admission to the changing rooms and pools. The *San Francisco Call* of August 1, 1897, reported what followed:

> On receiving the ticket, Mr. Harris presented the same at the proper place, and as he says, in a sober, orderly, polite and well-behaved manner, demanded the use of a bathing suit and a dressing-room, intending to avail himself of the opportunities of the bathing pools generally offered to patrons of the place, "but the defendant seeing and knowing that the plaintiff was a man of African descent, known as a negro and colored man," refused him the privileges for which he had paid. . . .
>
> When the refusal stated above took place, Mr. Harris says, he was in company with several white, or Caucasian friends, and his sensibilities and feelings were injured by the acts of the defendant in holding him up in the presence of his friends as of an inferior and degraded race.
>
> On the 11th of July Mr. Harris made another effort to enjoy the bathing facilities offered by Mr. Sutro, but he was again similarly rebuffed. He assesses his damages at $5,000 for each refusal, and consequently demands that Mr. Sutro pay him $10,000.

FOR ADVENTUROUS SWIMMERS, THERE WERE TRAPEZES, SLIDES, RINGS, AND A VARIETY OF DIVING BOARDS.

IN THIS CIRCA 1910 VIEW, BOTH POOLS #2 AND #3 HAVE BEEN PLANKED OVER.
THREE HIGH-DIVING PLATFORMS CAN BE SEEN AGAINST THE WALL AT FAR LEFT.
SINCE THE WATER WAS JUST 9½ FEET DEEP, THESE WERE USED ONLY BY PROFESSIONAL
DIVERS AND THE MOST ADVENTUROUS (OR FOOLHARDY) SWIMMERS.

A TINTYPE GALLERY AND A TOBACCO STORE FLANKED THE MAIN ENTRANCE ON POINT LOBOS AVENUE. THE FIRTH WHEEL RISES IN THE BACKGROUND.

In response to the *Call* story, Sutro Baths Superintendent A. O. Harrison attempted to clarify the Baths' policy: "Negroes," he said, "so long as they are sober and well behaved are allowed to enter the baths as spectators, but are not permitted to go in the water. It is not a matter of personal feeling with us but of business necessity. It would ruin our baths here because the white people would refuse to use them if the negroes were allowed equal privileges in that way. No one could in equity expect us to make such a sacrifice. I do not think such a case could ever be won against us. Public sentiment would be too strongly in opposition for any law to force such a commingling of the white and colored races."

Harrison went on to note that in the fifteen months the Baths had been open, no other "colored person attempted to mingle with the whites in the water." Despite Harrison's opinion, the suit went to trial.

On February 17, 1898, the *San Francisco Chronicle* announced the suit's conclusion. With Sutro's only defense being the objections of white patrons and resulting business loss, the judge instructed the jury that it must rule in favor of Harris by law. The jury awarded the minimum penalty of $50 for each of the two violations set forth in the complaint. It was a pyrrhic victory for Harris, since any verdict under $300 required the plaintiff to pay the

A TRANQUIL MOMENT ON A RESTAURANT BALCONY OVERLOOKING THE MAIN POOL.

costs of the trial. The *Chronicle* concluded that "after paying his attorneys [Harris] will be little or nothing ahead by the suit."

Economics of another sort were a continuing concern for the Baths, as visitation rarely rose above the break-even point. While more than 8,000 patrons might enter on a nice weekend day, during the week, use averaged about 500 bathers a day. At 25 cents per swimmer, the Baths grossed only about $4,500 a week.[33]

ADOLPH SUTRO died in 1898, leaving his eldest daughter, Dr. Emma Sutro Merritt, executrix of his estate. She quickly realized that despite her father's extensive landholdings, he had invested far too heavily in building his Cliff House, Baths, and streetcar line, and the estate was overextended. She began to unload unprofitable holdings. One of the first things she did was shut down the amusement zone along Merrie Way and, in 1899, sell off the Sutro Railroad Company.

In 1910, an appraisal of the Adolph Sutro Estate indicated that the estimated total value of the Baths (exclusive of machinery and equipment) was between $650,000 and $656,000. Dr. Merritt put the value at closer to $1 million. At the time, profits were averaging only $12,000 annually.

The appraiser described the Baths with an accountant's eye: "It is unfortunate that this structure, which is one of the 'Wonders of the West,' does not make a better showing from the standpoint of profit. The enterprise of the founder of this monumental structure has not been rewarded, except, perhaps to the extent of a grateful public." [34]

During the years that followed, Dr. Merritt tried repeatedly (and unsuccessfully) to sell the Baths. A 1912 bond measure directing the city to purchase the structure for $687,000 failed at the polls. She reduced the price, and in 1919, tried to get an investor to purchase the Baths for $410,000. Still no takers. The Baths and its aging collection of taxidermy displays and mummies would remain the property of the Sutro family until 1952.

SUTRO BATHS underwent few physical changes during its first four decades of operation. Photographs taken between 1896 and 1933 reveal only minor alterations to the building, such as a reduction in the height of the powerhouse smokestack and the addition of much-needed fire exits. In 1904, fuel oil replaced coal in the boilers. Also, the building's lighting system was upgraded and the entire complex converted to Pacific Gas and Electric service in 1912, after which the steam boilers served primarily to heat seawater for the swimming tanks.

Most exterior alterations focused on the seawall on the west side of the main Baths building and the causeway to Fisherman's Rock, which continued to suffer wave damage. In June 1905, a series of storms undermined it and eventually caused it to collapse, forcing Dr. Merritt to ask the estate for $30,000 to make neces-sary repairs. The problems with the causeway, it appears, had been going on for some time. Manager Harrison was quoted in the papers as saying, "A year ago the railroad leading from the quarry at the back of the Baths was injured by the storms . . . though so far there has been no actual damage to the Baths."[35] Photos of the Baths' exterior taken at the time document an increasingly undermined causeway and sea-wall; some show broken rail tracks dangling in mid-air.

Around 1910, the original rock causeway was replaced with a reinforced concrete jetty. About the same time, a small concrete patio was added outside the Baths' west wall near the head of the causeway. One historical photograph shows swimmers relaxing on this patio, suggesting that it may have been an early attempt at creating an outdoor sunbathing area, although one would be hard pressed to think of a less pleasant setting.

Where's Adolph?

Adolph Sutro's cremains were first entombed in a San Francisco cemetery near Lone Mountain. According to knowledgeable sources, his ashes were later spirited away and returned to Sutro Heights; his final resting spot remains a family secret.

A 1930S POSTCARD OF THE CLIFF HOUSE SHOWS A STONE URN (BOTTOM CENTER) THAT SOME BELIEVE HELD THE ASHES OF ADOLPH SUTRO. OTHERS SPECULATE IT WAS MERELY A RECYCLED FUNERARY DECORATION. RECOVERED IN THE 1980S, THE URN WAS TAKEN TO A LOCAL MORTUARY, FROM WHICH IT SUBSEQUENTLY DISAPPEARED.

Sutro Baths opened during the Victorian era, and for many years, even men's swimsuits featured modesty skirts. Curiously, the only person in this group portrait not ready to hit the water is the Life Saver, who's wearing a sweater, trousers, and shoes.

Sutro Baths and Pleasure Grounds

Admit to _____

Number _____

San Francisco, _____ 1896

Compliments of _____

"A Fishhook in the Desert": The End of Merrie Way

On March 14, 1911, a story in the San Francisco Call *chronicled the removal of the Firth Wheel, the last surviving attraction from Adolph Sutro's vanished pleasure grounds on Merrie Way. Although less than twenty years old, the Wheel had become symbolic of Sutro's fading seaside empire.*

JUNKMAN AT LAST GETS FIRTH WHEEL AT CLIFF

Relic of Midwinter Fair Will Be Torn Down Today

The Firth wheel, the circular and rusty monument of the Midwinter fair, which has stood on the bluff near Sutro's baths, is to be overturned today and reduced to junk. The old wheel was damaged by a storm a fortnight ago. The clutches were broken so that the wheel revolved in the windstorm. It can be of no possible use as a wheel and may serve some purpose as junk, so will be torn down.

The Firth wheel, built in imitation of the monster Ferris wheel, the sensation of the world's fair at Chicago, was one of the popular attractions at the Midwinter fair in 1894. At the conclusion of that exposition the wheel, with a number of other concession structures, was removed to the vicinity of the Cliff house, where a perpetual midway was to have been established. The investment was not profitable, and the wheel has stood out on the cliff, of no more use than a fishhook in a desert.

The Pleasure Grounds featured rides and midway attractions purchased from the 1894 Midwinter Fair.

THE SUTRO BATHS, SAN FRANCISCO, CALIFORNIA.—Drawn by CHARLES GRAHAM.—[See Page 545.]
The largest Salt-water Baths in the World.

Sutro Baths, San Francisco. Largest Bathing Establishment in the World.

I met her out at Sutro Baths.
I said "You swim like a duck."
She said." O! you're making game
of me."

No. 214.

Sutro Baths, Cliff House,
San Francisco, California

Interior Sutro Baths, San Francisco, California.

SIX
Sutro's in the News

THE SAN FRANCISCO PRESS regularly covered goings-on at Sutro's and the Cliff. Usually, the news was upbeat—the results of swimming competitions or the music program for weekend concerts. Sometimes, however, the subject matter turned dark. Following is a sampling of clippings culled from the archives of the *San Francisco Call*.

April 4, 1896
CLIFTON BROKE HIS NOSE
THE GAY HORSEMAN'S FATE ON A CHUTE AT SUTRO BATHS
He Slid Face Downward and Bumped Upon the Bottom Curve—
Worse Than a Polo Hurdle

Talbot Clifton, the horseman and eccentric capitalist of Burlingame, is once more in trouble. This time it is nothing more serious than a broken nose, which "my lud" is nursing with mingled sensations of adhesive plaster and disquieting reflections of his latest ambition to be an athlete and one of the boys.

   He vows that never again shall he essay a plunge into a bath from one of these newfangled sliding-boards, the use of which has proved disastrous to his lordly dignity and incidentally to his olfactory organ.

Clifton paid a visit to the Sutro Baths Thursday night. A few of his intimates accompanied him and the ubiquitous valet, who is better known in Clifton's haunts as "me man."

The promenade and the vastness of the building, with its novelties, its swimming tanks and its louvre [sic] fascinated Clifton, who soon became absorbed in the bathers. Riding the water hobby-horses, plunging, diving and above all shooting the green, glass chutes appears to be the acme of sport in his eyes; and he resolved to try them all.

"Fetch in a bathing suit, me man," he exclaimed, delving into a long purse for a dollar.

The valet secured a suit and presently Talbot appeared from a dressing-room in all his athletic magnificence. Of course, the crowd admired hard and fast and the English nobleman wished to be at his best. Sliding down the inclined boards seemed as easy as taking a polo hurdle, and at worst one could only come to the bottom. Nothing was so commonplace as shooting downward feet first. Then again Clifton is nothing if not original. So he slid away headfirst and face downward. It was this that caused all the trouble.

Clifton forgot that there was a curve at the bottom of the chute, placed there for the purpose of shooting bathers outward over the water, and when his forward section reached the curve his prominent nose was in the way. It struck the plank and Clifton fell in a lump into the water, with a ruddy glow about him. When he appeared above the water consternation reigned.

"I broke me nose!" yelled my lord. "I broke me nose! Hi! Where's me man?"

The man was beside the tank instantly.

"Call a doctor. I broke me nose." The physician was summoned, and after some delay Clifton was patched up sufficiently to be able to reach his rooms.

May 3, 1896

MAYOR SUTRO IS SUED
RESULT OF AN ACCIDENT AT THE BATHS DUE TO A MISLEADING SIGN
Frank Bowers Made a Dive and Found the Bottom Quicker Than He Expected

The first suit against the Sutro baths for injuries sustained by a bather was filed in the Justices' Court Friday by Attorney James P. Sweeny for Frank Bowers.

The complaint alleges that Bowers is an "experienced swimmer, diver and all-around aquatic expert," and that by the carelessness and negligence of Adolph

Sutro, the owner of the baths, he was seriously injured by coming into contact with the bottom of the swimming tank while engaged in natatorial pursuits.

Bowers' story is that on April 3 last he went to the Sutro baths, and after paying for a suit went to the tank for a swim. Being an expert diver he mounted one of the platforms where a sign indicated the water was six feet deep, and he plunged off. He came into violent contact with the bottom of the tank, and was so seriously bruised about his head and shoulders that he was compelled to seek the services of a physician.

He states that immediately after leaving the water he measured the depth of the same at the point where he plunged off, and found that instead of six feet the water was only four and a half feet deep, and that his injuries were due to the negligence of the management in not having the proper depth stated on the sign boards.

He asks for $299 damages and costs of suit.

THEY BLAME MR. SUTRO
Coroner's Jury Returned a Sharp Verdict Concerning Frank Denvir's Death
The Management of the Baths Censured for Not Keeping the Tanks Full of Water

The management of Sutro baths was strongly censured by a Coroner's jury yesterday for the death of Frank Denvir, who fractured his skull by falling into an empty tank while preparing to take a plunge into one of the smaller reservoirs.

On July 8 young Denvir with several companions visited the Cliff House resort to enjoy a swim in the Mayor's expensive bathing establishment. While in the act of climbing a ladder leading to one of the chutes his foot slipped, causing him to fall backward into the large tank. This was empty, and Denvir struck on the hard cement, receiving a fracture of the skull, from the effects of which he died a few hours later.

Ten witnesses were called to testify at the inquest, and with but one or two exceptions they agreed that the ladder, as well as the platform on which it rested, was entirely unprotected so far as guide ropes or railing went, and when the tanks were empty the public was in constant danger.

Professor Killick, the swimming instructor at the baths, said that due care had been exercised to prevent accidents, and testified that a rope had been stretched across the platform from which the boy fell. By the same witness, however, it was shown that the rope extended only from one side of the platform and as a guard was entirely useless. Other witnesses testifying substantially to the same facts were: Dr. Hunkeu, C. W. Freese, Mrs. Rose Chapman and C. L. Hanke. The latter was with Denvir at the time of the accident. He said that he was going up the ladder just in advance of the deceased, when his foot slipped against Denvir, knocking him from his position to the cement flooring below.

The jury retired and after a few minutes returned the following verdict: And we further find from the evidence presented that the deceased came to his death by accident, caused by a fall in an empty tank, and we, the jury, strongly censure the management of Sutro's Baths for not having a proper depth of water in the tank in which the deceased met his death, and we further censure the management for not having a proper depth of water in all tanks while the baths are in public use. [Jury] C. M. Daiss (foreman), Philip J. Plunkeith, W. R. Pease, John J. Mackey, Charles Tyson, M. Kearney, L. Joiner.

May 22, 1897

ADOLPH SUTRO SUED

William Denvir has sued Adolph Sutro for $50,000 damages on account of the death of his minor son Francis, who was accidentally killed at the Sutro baths on the 8th of last July. The boy fell into a tank that was left empty. The plaintiff alleges neglect on the part of Mr. Sutro's employees.

December 27, 1897

BROKE HIS LEG AT PLAY

Frank Tully Injured at the Sutro Scenic Railway

Frank Tully, a young man who lives with his parents at 431½ Clementina street, broke his right leg below the knee yesterday afternoon while riding on the deserted scenic railway near Sutro's Baths.

He, in company with Monte Lipman, left the baths and strolled around in search of pleasure and finally discovered the railway. They pulled the car to the top and started down the slide, but unfortunately for them a small boy had placed a stick across the track. When about half way down they ran into the obstruction and the boys were thrown to the front of the car.

Tully's leg was broken and Lipman, who lives at 37 Langton Street, was severely bruised about the right leg and hip. Both boys were treated at the Receiving Hospital and afterward sent to their homes.

THE WATER WAS SHALLOW

H. S. Werner has commenced suit against Adolph Sutro to recover $10,000 for personal injuries received at Sutro's Baths on the 6th ult. The plaintiff alleges that he sprang from a springboard, fitted for diving purposes, into one of the tanks, and as the water was not of sufficient depth he struck his head on the bottom and permanently injured himself. He contends that the accident was due to the carelessness of the defendant, and he sues to recover.

HIGH DIVER STRIKES SWIMMER AT SUTRO'S

Eric Muhr Comes Down From Great Height Upon Head of J. H. Griggs

Eric Muhr of 230 O'Farrell street was at Sutro Baths yesterday afternoon, doing a few high diving stunts.

He had dived from the lower altitudes and, as his courage rose with each dive, he mounted to the highest platform.

J. H. Griggs, a teamster of 305 Turk Street, happened to be swimming through the water at the very spot in which Muhr wanted to land on his last high dive. Muhr came down with terrific force, his back striking against Griggs' head. Both were badly injured. Muhr was sent to the Park Receiving Hospital, while Griggs, whose injuries were of a more serious nature, was taken to the French Hospital, the latter being nearer the scene of the accident. Dr. Boscowitz treated Muhr and found that he had sustained a contusion of the back and left side, not serious. Griggs was found to have sustained a concussion of the brain, with internal injuries. Both will recover.

INJURED WHILE BATHING

Hans Georgeuson, a sailor, residing at 228 East Street, lies at the point of death at the Park Hospital from injuries received while bathing at Sutro Baths yesterday afternoon. Georgeuson dove into shallow water and struck his head against the cement bottom, fracturing his skull.

June 28, 1908

BATHERS COLLIDE ON SLIDE

John Formal of 100 Pierce street started head first to "shoot the chutes" into the cooling pool at the Sutro Baths yesterday. He was almost there when another eager bather slid into him from behind and nearly knocked his feet through his spine. Forman was so completely taken by surprise that he found himself unable to swim and would have drowned if a rescue party formed in a hurry hadn't dived and brought him to the surface.

March 17, 1912

YOUTH STRICKEN WHILE IN POOL

Son of Emporium Department Manager Loses Life While Swimming in Baths

Ruben Henry Levy, an electrician who lived at 1621 Masonic Avenue, was drowned in the Sutro Baths yesterday afternoon. Levy, who was 21 years old, went to the baths accompanied by his brother, Clarence, and his two sisters. The young man entered the warm water tank at 1:45 p.m. and at 2:30 his body was found by J. T. Hilzinger, an employe [sic] of the baths.

Efforts were made to resusciate [sic] the drowned man, but after an hour's work on the part of Hilzinger and J. W. S. McGregor, swimming instructor, the task was abandoned, Dr. Lee W. Burt of Los Angeles pronouncing the man dead.

Hilzinger found Levy clinging to the railing with his head partly under water. The victim was frothing at the mouth, and this leads to the belief that he was stricken with epilepsy. Levy was the son of J. T. Levy, manager of the business department of the Emporium. Permission was given for the young man's relatives to remove his body to an undertaking establishment.

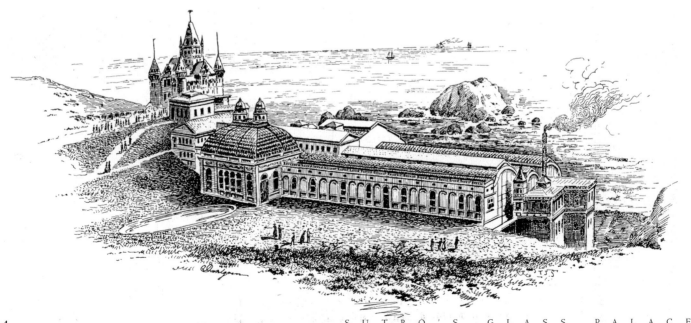

Murder at the Baths?

On March 15, 1908, attendants at Sutro Baths found a dead body at the bottom of one of the swimming tanks. The sensationally bent San Francisco Chronicle *gave extensive coverage to what was initially thought to be the Bath's first crime.*

BATHER'S DEATH DARK MYSTERY
UNKNOWN'S BODY FISHED FROM TANK AT THE SUTRO BATHS
Flesh Torn and Bruised—All Indications Tend to Point Toward a Theory of Murder

The police and Coroner Leland are hard at work trying to solve the mystery surrounding the finding of the body of an unknown bather in tank 6, better known as the small tank at the Sutro Baths, yesterday about noon. The body was discovered lying on the concrete floor of the tank by Attendant Peter Palengat, and the latter at once notified other employes [sic], and it was lifted from four feet of water. A hurry call was sent in for the Park Emergency ambulance, as it was thought that life was not extinct.

When Steward Saunders of the Park Emergency Hospital arrived he said there was no life, and the Morgue was notified and removed the body. At the Morgue, where Coroner Leland examined the remains, he said the case was one which called for the most careful investigation by the police. The body was covered with bruises and abrasions from head to foot, yet the strangest part of the whole affair is that nobody at the bathing place heard any screams or knew of any scuffle. Even the attendant who must have roomed the unknown, Louis Stolle, could not identify the body when it was taken from the tank.

ABRASIONS ON HEAD
On the right side of the head there are five abrasions, each at least an inch in length and fully one-quarter of an inch in width. There are two well-defined marks on the chin below the neck, which look very much as though they were given by some person who might have choked the man in life. Patches of skin have been torn from the right arm, both legs and the left thigh.

As the body was found lying at the bottom of the tank face upwards, Coroner Leland says he cannot understand how the marks on the chin could have been produced even if the man fell into the tank or died from cramps or apoplexy. While the Coroner is unprepared to say that he thinks a murder has been committed, he agrees with Captain Kelly of the detective department that the circumstances surround the finding of the body are very mysterious. Both say a thorough investigation must be made. First both the Coroner and the police will try to establish the identity of the body.

CLOSE INVESTIGATION MADE
Superintendent A. O. Harrison of the Sutro Baths is aiding the authorities in every manner possible. He closely questioned all the attendants, but no one,

even the woman ticket seller, can remember the time the unknown entered the bathhouse. All agree that the man could not have come in very much before 11 o'clock, because Attendant Stolle, in whose department the man roomed, remembers that he roomed but one person yesterday morning and that was about 11 o'clock.

Still more mystery is thrown around the affair by the fact that tank 6, in which the body was found, was roped off, and guards informed bathers that the tank was not ready to receive swimmers. The tank was roped off yesterday morning at 7 o'clock thoroughly empty. Half an hour later water was turned into it, and it was the intention to have it filled by 1 o'clock yesterday afternoon for bathers. When filled this tank never contains more than four and a half feet of water. It is the tank generally used by children and beginners in learning to swim.

No Noises Are Heard

No attendants or bathers remember hearing any noise or seeing any scuffle about tank 6 yesterday morning, Superintendent Harrison informed Coroner Leland yesterday that at the time the body was found in the tank the place was well filled with bathers in tanks 3, 4, and 5.

The body at the Morgue is that of a man who would weigh between 145 and 150 pounds, and is five feet seven inches tall. The hair is curly brown and the moustache is sandy. He would be about 40 years. The clothing is made up of a black coat and vest, white and gray striped trousers, soft brown shirt, blue stock-ings, a brown derby hat and black lace shoes. The hat-band bears the initials "J.H.S."

The property found in the pockets of the clothing included one key, a knife, 5 cents in cash, one cheap comb and a button hook bearing the inscription, "Crawford's shoe store." On the middle finger of the right hand was a gold ring with a pink stone.

The inquest into the death will be deferred by Coroner Leland until such time as the police have made a careful and searching investigation.

March 16

SUTRO BATHS CASE BAFFLES THE POLICE

Mystery Veils Death of Unknown Found in Swimming Tank

Although Detective Purcell and other policemen from the Park Station are endeavoring to solve the mystery surrounding the finding of the body of an unknown at the Sutro Baths on Saturday, nothing has been learned which will aid Coroner Leland in unraveling the tangle.

Yesterday morning at 10 o'clock Dr. Clark held an autopsy, and reported that death was due to asphyxiation from submersion, the lungs being filled with water.

Steward Saunders of the Park Emergency Hospital says positively that no water came from the mouth when he reached the bathhouse and examined the body on Saturday afternoon.

Coroner Leland is of the same opinion he expressed on Saturday afternoon, to the effect that the case presented some very peculiar situations, but Deputy Sam Cronin and Messenger Richard Carrick who removed the body from the bathhouse to the Morgue, incline to the opinion that the man either fell into the tank unobserved, or was attacked by cramps after going into the pool.

On the other hand, tank No. 6, where the body was found, was roped off, and bathers were warned not to enter it. The bathhouse attendants contend that it was possible that the body was sucked through one of the drain pipes from one pool to another. No such accident, however, [has] happened before in the history of the baths.

The inquest will be delayed until the police make a very careful investigation. No stone will be left unturned to identify the body, in the hope that identification may lead to some clew [sic] upon which the detectives can work.

The next day, March 17, the San Francisco Call *provided the somewhat anticlimactic "rest of the story."*

DEAD MAN IDENTIFIED

The man who was found dead at the Sutro Baths last Saturday was yesterday identified as Jacob Svitka, a tailor at 934 Oak Street. An investigation disclosed that Svitka was suffering from a weak heart and death, it is thought, was due to this cause.

So how did Svitka's badly bruised body end up in a closed pool? Although never confirmed, the most likely scenario was the one proposed by the attendants: that Svitka died in one tank, sank to the bottom, and his body was sucked into tank six through a connecting pipe while it was being filled.

The Tropic Beach featured palm-frond cabanas and fabric clouds suspended from the rafters.

SEVEN
Modernizing the Baths

A PARTY AT THE TROPIC BEACH, CIRCA 1935.

THE AGING BATHS received a major makeover in the mid-1930s, when the Sutro Estate, which still owned the building, gave its exterior a facelift and added new recreation facilities. The project involved rebuilding the main pool, modernizing the Greek Temple entrance, creating outdoor picnic grounds, upgrading the power plant, and converting a portion of the interior into an indoor ice skating rink.

Carried out under the direction of manager Adolph G. Sutro, the late mayor's grandson, the upgrades were an attempt to revitalize the Baths and attract a new (and younger) clientele. In addition to physical alterations, a publicity campaign touted the health benefits of swimming at Sutro Baths, while colorful brochures promoted the building as a unique venue for parties, dancing, and even group picnics and barbeques.

Swimming Tanks

From its opening in the 1890s, Sutro Baths incorporated seven swimming tanks: the L-shaped main tank (Tank #1), five rectangular tanks (Tanks #2 through #6), and a small oval tank at the foot of the grand staircase called the plunge.

During the 1934–1935 renovations, the main tank was drastically reduced in size by the construction of a new 15-foot-deep diving tank at its north end, and again when a new recreation area—the Tropic Beach—was built in its south dogleg.

The original deep end of the main tank was only 9½ feet, which presented a hazard for any swimmer courageous (or foolhardy) enough to attempt dives from the higher diving platforms. In order to create a more suitable diving area, a deeper pool was built at the north end of the existing main tank. Constructed of reinforced concrete, it was essentially a freestanding structure within the walls of the original main tank. The new tank was 28 feet wide, 60 feet long, and 15 feet deep, and featured four diving boards and two elevated diving platforms attached to the building's walls, the highest of which was 45 feet above the water. This new pool was designated Tank #7.

At the same time the new diving tank was being built, the dogleg of the former main tank was walled off and drained. The reclaimed pool bottom was partially filled with imported sand to create the "Tropic Beach," which featured fake palm trees, stuffed monkeys, cabanas, ping-pong tables, shuffleboard courts, and lounge chairs. Parachute-type fabric draped from the ceiling trusses and pillars attempted to suggest clouds floating overhead.

All this new construction left the main pool 100 feet shorter. The truncated center section remained in use, however, and was upgraded with a floating water wheel and new, longer slides. To lessen the visual impact of the vertical walls of the new diving tank, a seascape mural was painted on the side facing the main tank.[36]

Across the way, two of the four original small pools were planked over and converted to volleyball courts. Chicken-wire enclosures around the courts kept stray balls from landing in the nearby pools and on the Tropic Beach.

Behind the scenes, infrastructure upgrades included new filtration tanks and other mechanical improvements inside the powerhouse.

Entrance Façade

The original Greek Temple pedestrian entrance on Point Lobos Avenue received a facelift during 1933–1934 with the addition of a whimsical façade that combined elements of Art Deco and Coney Island honky-tonk. Designed by San Francisco architect Harold G. Stoner, it was said to have been inspired by the modernistic architecture of the 1933 "Century of Progress" Chicago World's Fair. However, even a casual observer could still discern the 1894 Greek Temple barely hidden behind the street-side Arabian Nights portico.

Sutro Baths
San Francisco

Ian 400

THE REMODELED MAIN ENTRANCE WAS PAINTED IN VIVID
COLORS.

RESTAURANTS AND SOUVENIR SHOPS LINED POINT LOBOS
AVENUE WEST OF SUTRO'S.

In 1937, an ice rink was constructed over the former Tropic Beach. The wall with the alpine mural separated the rink from the swimming pools. The photo above was taken from the same viewpoint as the photo on page 98.

Ice Rink

The Tropic Beach was never really a success. Despite the garland-wrapped iron columns and faux palm fronds, the overall effect was very much like partying in a drained swimming pool—which it was. In 1937, the Tropic Beach was removed and a new ice rink took its place.

Contrary to popular belief, the ice rink was not a frozen-over portion of the swimming tank. Instead, the rink was elevated about 10 feet above the bottom of the drained tank, supported by an array of sturdy wood columns set into the original tank floor. The open area beneath the rink allowed workers to access the intricate refrigeration system that kept its surface frozen.

There were other engineering challenges. The dogleg of the original main tank had featured three columns that supported the roof. These had to be removed to make way for the ice rink, and in their place, large steel cantilevered girders were installed to support the roof over the rink. The overhead glass roof panels were another problem. Unfiltered sunlight streaming through the glass would have melted the ice, so the glass ceiling panels directly over the ice were either painted over or covered with tarpaper to make them opaque. This made the rink quite dark, which required the installation of a new system of floodlights to illuminate the ice. (The west-facing windows were left clear, though, and the late afternoon sun would beam through during wintertime and produce puddles in the northwest portion of the rink.[37])

Other changes included refrigeration equipment in the powerhouse and a wooden addition for skaters' lockers and changing rooms atop the concrete patio outside the western wall. Beneath the bleachers, a skate shop and clubrooms for skate teams were created in the former swimmers' changing rooms.

In an attempt to isolate the ice rink within the Baths, a floor-to-ceiling plywood wall was built to separate the rink from the adjacent tanks. Apparently, this was intended to minimize condensation problems arising from the proximity of the large expanse of ice to the heated saltwater pools. Still, one visitor recalled that when conditions were right, fog would occasionally form inside Sutro Baths.[38]

EIGHT
The Whitney Era

IN 1952, THE SUTRO ESTATE announced once again that it would have to close Sutro Baths, with a final date of September 1, 1952. Newspapers lamented the passing of "the great old lady," but no one seemed to have the ability—or the desire—to stop the inevitable.

At the last minute, a buyer emerged: George Whitney, owner of nearby Playland at the Beach and the Cliff House, known as the "P. T. Barnum of the Golden Gate." Whitney purchased the Baths from the Sutro heirs on September 1, 1952, for $250,000, a fraction of what Adolph Sutro had paid to build the establishment sixty years previous.

During the ensuing years, Whitney reinvented Sutro Baths as a sort of Gay '90s theme park, turning much of the interior into a museum for his own artifacts and curios. And Whitney had a lot to display.

"MRS. ITO," A LIFE-SIZE CARVING OF A JAPANESE WOMAN, WAS ONE OF THE MANY ATTRACTIONS DISPLAYED BY GEORGE WHITNEY.

(OPPOSITE, TOP) PHOTOS FROM THE 1940S REVEAL THE COLOR PALETTE INSIDE SUTRO'S. THIS VIEW SHOWS THE NEW DIVING TANK AT UPPER LEFT.

(LOWER LEFT) BY THE 1940S, SWIMMERS WERE ALLOWED TO WEAR THEIR OWN SUITS.

(LOWER RIGHT) THE ICE RINK APPEARS UNNATURALLY DARK IN THIS VIEW, TAKEN WITH THE OVERHEAD LIGHTS TURNED OFF.

George K. Whitney, owner of Playland at the Beach and the Cliff House, was known as the "P. T. Barnum of the Golden Gate."

The main entrance staircase featured promotional cards for the dizzying array of Whitney-era attractions on display below.

Whitney was a collector of collections, with a weakness for estate auctions, and his extensive and eclectic holdings included horse-drawn buggies, spinning wheels, antique photographs, early bicycles, suits of armor, coin-operated orchestrions and peep shows, and other wonderfully odd items that had caught his attention. He decided that Sutro's was the perfect place to display his treasures, much in the same way that Adolph Sutro himself had used the vast interior to display his "bric-a-brac" (Sutro's term) when the Baths first opened.

ELABORATE STREET-SCENE TABLEAUS CAME ALIVE AT THE DROP OF A COIN.

One of the first things Whitney did upon acquiring Sutro's was to clean house. Many of the items Adolph Sutro had originally put on display had suffered greatly over the years from leaky roofs and steamy salt air, especially the taxidermy specimens, and Whitney ordered most of them carted off to landfill. He retained only the most valuable of Adolph Sutro's original museum pieces, which included the Egyptian collection with its several original mummies, sarcophagi, and funerary objects.

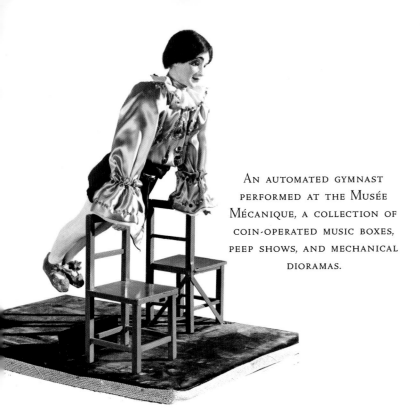

An automated gymnast performed at the Musée Mécanique, a collection of coin-operated music boxes, peep shows, and mechanical dioramas.

Also, America's tastes in recreation were changing. Sutro Baths had been a major destination for the 1890s streetcar crowd, but automobiles were ascendant in post-WWII America. Those who wanted to spend a day swimming and sunning were increasingly likely to drive north to the Russian River or south to Santa Cruz rather than head to Sutro's.

On January 1, 1954, barely a year after purchasing Sutro Baths, Whitney closed the tanks forever. From that point onward, ice skating and arcade attractions would be the primary recreational activities; everything, including Whitney's displays of curios, was contained within the southern half of the building, closest to Point Lobos Avenue. The drained tanks and changing rooms and the powerhouse were simply left to molder in the unused northern half of the structure, an area the Whitney family referred to as "the back property."[39]

The Sky Tram

The Sky Tram, built 1954–1955, was the last attempt by George Whitney to create a modern attraction at the Cliff House–Sutro Baths area. Although not phys-

Whitney also remodeled the Point Lobos entrance once again, this time skinning over the 1930s Art Deco façade with a redwood exterior done in the then-popular Modern style. Blazoned across the entrance was Whitney's new tag line: "Fabulous Sutro's—Since 1896." Notably absent was the word "Baths."

The pools did not fare well under Whitney. Although when he purchased the Baths, he had grandly announced that the pools would remain open, grim economics soon revealed that they were a losing proposition. The aging concrete tanks and mildewing locker rooms could not compete with the modern swimming pools and recreation centers being built around the city by San Francisco's Recreation and Park Department.

ically connected to the Baths, the ride brought many changes to Point Lobos when the catch basin and tunnels that originally filled the Baths were converted to attractions for passengers on the aerial ride.

A streamlined tramcar suspended from overhead cables transported passengers from the observation deck behind the Cliff House to a new overlook constructed at the tip of Point Lobos. According to George Whitney, Jr., his family had worked as consultants to Walt Disney on the development of Disneyland, and the Sky Tram borrowed many of its design features from the rides being built at the super new amusement park in Anaheim.[40]

To entice visitors, Whitney capitalized on several nearby shipwreck sites and christened the new overlook at Point Lobos "Shipwreck Point." (Most of the wrecks had actually disintegrated years before, but Whitney was a showman, not a historian.) After taking the one-way trip to Shipwreck Point, disembarking visitors could look (usually in vain) for the promised shipwrecks, watch the waves break into Sutro's catch basin, or descend a steep staircase to a lower level and explore two of the tunnels associated with Sutro Baths.

The overlook also featured two artificial waterfalls that cascaded in two stages down the face of the cliff on the south side of the point. Not one to underplay anything, Whitney touted them as the "largest salt-water waterfalls in the world."

The ride, never economically successful, was hampered by the tram's slow rate of travel and the limited number of passengers it could carry per trip. In addi-

AN AERIAL VIEW OF THE SKY TRAM, WHICH VAGUELY RESEMBLED A STREAMLINED TRAILER, MAKING ITS SLOW JOURNEY PAST SUTRO BATHS.

tion, the ride simply took visitors out and back; there was no opportunity for two-way fares. The Sky Tram closed in 1965.

NINE
The End and a New Beginning

GEORGE WHITNEY DIED IN 1958, but his family continued to operate his holdings, including Sutro's, for another eight years. Throughout this period, the old structure, exposed to endless blasts of Pacific wind and water, continued to deteriorate. Whitney's maintenance personnel, overwhelmed by the scale of the place, essentially abandoned the north half of the building and its empty swimming tanks to the ravages of the weather and the destructive energies of young boys.

(ABOVE) THE POINT LOBOS ENTRANCE UNDER THE WHITNEYS. THE CANOPY AND GLASS PANELS FROM THE 1930S ART DECO EXTERIOR WERE INCORPORATED INTO THIS MID-CENTURY MODERN FAÇADE.

(OPPOSITE) AN AERIAL VIEW OF SUTRO'S SHORTLY BEFORE CLOSING. THE RECTANGULAR BUILDING ON THE PLATEAU IN THE FOREGROUND WAS THE SKY TRAM STATION, WITH THE CATCH BASIN BELOW AND TO THE RIGHT.

In the early 1960s, the Whitney heirs decided to sell part of the Baths property to developer Robert Frasier, whose previous San Francisco projects included the widely criticized Fontana Apartments near Fisherman's Wharf. Frasier had big plans for his portion of the bowl-shaped cove, and floated proposals for residential and commercial developments; some renderings showed terraced condominiums along the cove's curved slopes, while others included high-rise apartments at the tip of Point Lobos. In all of his proposals, though, one fact was

(LEFT AND FACING PAGE) ARTISTS' CONCEPTIONS OF CONDOMINIUMS AND HIGH-RISES PROPOSED FOR THE SUTRO BATHS SITE, JANUARY 1965. SAN FRANCISCANS WERE APPALLED.

PRELIMINARY PLANS FOR CLIFF HOUSE PROPERTIES

obvious: not a trace of Sutro Baths would remain.

"Fabulous Sutro's" continued to operate from 1964 until 1966, with Robert Frasier and George Whitney, Jr., sharing ownership of the building; the wall separating the skating rink from the defunct pools was the dividing line between their properties. But the economics were unavoidable: Sutro's was continuing to lose money and the only apparent solution was to demolish the bathhouse and redevelop the cove.

Sutro's closed for business on March 1, 1966, and within a few days, workers began removing George Whitney's "collection of collections" to safe storage, where they would await eventual auction. (An exception was the Egyptian collection, which the Whitney heirs donated to San Francisco State University.) By late spring, the building was empty and the long and expensive process of demolition began. A plan briefly existed in which Frasier would demolish only the north half of Sutro's and redevelop that portion of the cove, while Whitney would retain the skating rink and keep it in operation. This scheme was never realized, though, and Whitney eventually sold his remaining interests to Frasier's Alexander Land Company.

Once Frasier owned the entire Baths building and cove, he quickly began to implement his vision of a "posh resort above Point Lobos, a group of apartment buildings between the resort and Point Lobos Avenue, and a shopping center and pedestrian mall on the site of the Sutro Baths." Aaron's Building Wrecking Company of Sacramento was awarded the contract, and demolition of the seventy-two-year-old bath-

PRELIMINARY PLANS FOR
CLIFF HOUSE PROPERTIES
SAN FRANCISCO, CALIFORNIA
27 JANUARY 1965
WURSTER, BERNARDI + EMMONS, ARCHITECTS

house began on June 12, 1966.

Two weeks later, on Sunday, June 26, 1966, a fire broke out in the partially dismantled structure. Pushed by heavy westerly winds, the fire quickly turned into a five-alarm inferno that engulfed the entire building. What would have taken weeks for wrecking crews to accomplish was finished by fire in a matter of hours. Sutro Baths was gone. In its place stood a black tangle of bent truss rods and iron columns, sparkling here and there with broken fragments of the glass that had covered the once-glorious structure.

Police and fire department investigations in the wake of the fire determined that the point of origin had been in a pile of old posters near the skating rink, and that arson had been the cause of the blaze. The prime suspect was a local youth with a past conviction for arson who had been hired as a watchman at the demolition site. (The wrecking company had laid him off after only a week, but then brought him back on June 26—the day the fire broke out.)

During the fire, a mounted policeman found the watchman running through the bushes near the conflagration, "perspiring freely and breathing heavily." He claimed he was chasing two juveniles who had started the fire, but could only provide the officer with vague descriptions. Detained by the San Francisco police, the watchman was questioned at length but eventually released for lack of evidence. Although never prosecuted, arson inspectors still consider him the only suspect.[41]

The National Park Service Steps In

The destruction of Sutro Baths corresponded with the dawning of a new preservation movement around the San Francisco Bay Area. Manifesting itself in many forms and locations during the 1960s ("Save the Bay," "No Growth," "The Freeway Revolt"), it was driven by the growing realization that urban landscapes and adjacent wild lands were being threatened by nonstop development. Preservation groups organized to protect resources ranging from tiny neighborhood parks to former dairy ranches in southern Marin County.

The ultimate manifestation of this preservation movement was the 1972 Congressional creation of the Golden Gate National Recreation Area (GGNRA), a unit of the National Park Service (NPS). The purpose of the sprawling new park was to preserve the natural, historic, and recreational values of lands extending from Marin County's Point Reyes on the north to San Mateo County beaches on the south. GGNRA's boundaries also sheltered many historic sites precious to generations of San Franciscans: the

Presidio of San Francisco, the Marin Headlands, Alcatraz Island, the Cliff House—and the ruins of Sutro Baths.

Park planners were careful to include the Baths site, even though it was private property, since it was a critical parcel in the unbroken greenbelt being assembled along the western edge of the San Francisco peninsula. Fortunately, Robert Frasier's firm had never been able to implement its plans for condominiums at the Sutro site; neighborhood opposition, funding problems, and coastal zoning regulations combined to stall his vision, allowing the land to remain undeveloped.

However, inclusion within GGNRA's borders did not automatically make Frasier's land the property of the US Government. Rather, it only authorized the National Park Service to purchase the land from its owners. By the time the NPS began negotiations, Frasier's development corporation had sold the Baths site to yet another owner, Mr. Zev Ben-Simon, who believed its value was $9.5 million—far more than the Park Service felt it was worth. In May 1980, following several years of negotiation, the NPS finally acquired the 4.4-acre site of the former Sutro Baths and adjacent hillsides for $5.5 million, saving the cove from commercial development forever.

Over the past three decades, little has been done to enhance the ruins of Sutro's glass palace. While the NPS has proposed various plans to install walkways with railings and interpretive waysides, improvements have been limited to safety barriers and warning signs. Visiting the site is still an adventure that

requires sturdy shoes and the navigation of steep roads, while understanding the ruins remains an exercise in self-taught industrial archeology.

Interestingly, most visitors seem to prefer that Sutro Baths be maintained in this state of arrested decay. While there have been occasional suggestions to rebuild the Baths (far too costly to seriously consider), the most common visitor feedback is simply to leave well enough alone and allow as much freedom as possible when exploring the site.

Alas, decay of the physical remains of the Baths is far from "arrested." One side of the semicircular 1880s aquarium has collapsed, and the concrete channels guiding water from the catch basin to the aquarium are also falling into the ocean. Features that were highly visible in the 1970s, such as foundations for the bleachers and grand staircase, are slowly collapsing due to coastal erosion. The swimming pools and original aquarium have been partially filled by material cascading down the hillsides, and the bowl-shaped cove is gradually filling with fresh water from hillside springs—the same springs tapped by Sutro to feed his boilers and fill his freshwater plunge.

With the filling and flooding of the pools, the cove now resembles photos of Sutro's Swimming Pond taken in the early 1890s, when the aquarium and rock seawall were the only human-made features on the beach. Today, though, the bathers are aquatic

(Above and opposite) The author took these photographs in October 1966 showing heavy equipment removing what was left of the Baths following the June fire.

seabirds and the occasional wandering otter.

Steps will need to be taken quickly if the Baths are to be preserved. Ignoring the situation is not an alternative, since another part of the NPS mandate is to protect the site for the enjoyment of future generations.

There is one point all agree upon, however: don't ruin the ruins.

At the time of this writing, the National Park Service is about to embark on a planning effort for safeguarding and interpreting the Sutro Baths site. The challenge will be to meet the dual mission of preserving the historic remnants at the cove and providing for visitor safety, while simultaneously maintaining the sense of mystery—and even a whiff of danger—that continues to draw visitors to Sutro's vanished glass palace. Only time will tell.

TRACES OF THE PAST
A Field Guide to the Ruins

SUTRO BATHS TODAY presents a jumbled array of concrete ruins, flooded foundations, and tunnels of various sizes piercing the flanks of Point Lobos. Making sense of these features can be a challenge.

The building that housed the Baths was an evolving structure that changed radically with the whims of Adolph Sutro, especially during the early years of construction. Only in its final form did it become the great wood-and-glass structure that many people still remember. The 1966 fire that destroyed the glass palace essentially revealed the earliest features of the embryonic baths: the original 1880s water-catchment system and aquarium, the 1890s rock seawall that enclosed Seal Rock Beach, and the remnants of the first concrete swimming tanks. Also visible today are a few utility features dating to the 1930s.

Archaeologists believe that many more features likely survive beneath the brackish waters and mud that now fill the ruins.

Catch Basin

Beginning in late 1884, when Sutro began constructing his artificial aquarium at the north end of the cove, a catch basin that would trap wave water and divert it to the circular tank was a key element. The artificial basin was carved from the west side of Point Lobos (or Parallel Point, as it was often called) at an elevation of 17 feet—3 feet higher than the water level inside the aquarium—which ensured a constant gravity flow from the basin to the tank. Sutro's employees and the newspapers had several names for this basin, all of which in some way described its basic function.

The catch basin was greatly enlarged over the years, the result of Sutro's workers continually quarrying rock at the point. The earliest published description of the basin appeared in an article in the September 4, 1886, *San Francisco Morning Call*, which described its dimensions as 72 feet long by 20 feet wide. If accurate, the catch basin was significantly smaller then, since today it measures approximately 110 feet long by 50 wide, an increase in area of 380 percent.

Main Tunnel/Main Canal

The main tunnel originally led from the catch basin to the aquarium, and was one of the first structures Adolph Sutro's workers built (or rather, excavated) through Point Lobos. Originally nearly 200 feet long, the tunnel's length was repeatedly nibbled away by quarrying operations at the point. In some places, workers dug away the overhead rock entirely and effectively turned the tunnel into an open canal for much of its length.

The channel was lined with concrete, and starting in the early 1890s, construction reports alternately refer to it as both a tunnel and a canal. (Both terms were correct.) Today, the main tunnel begins as a rock passageway at the catch basin, emerges briefly into sunlight where a massive sluice gate was once sited, then reenters a concrete-lined cave before emerging near the old aquarium.

Backup Pump Tunnel

It was obvious to Sutro that wave action alone couldn't be relied upon to fill the Baths, especially during low tides and on calm days. He decided a backup pump (sometimes called a circulating pump) was needed, and had one installed inside a special room excavated within the rocky headlands of Parallel Point. Here, in a chamber 14 feet below the level of the catch basin, a steam-powered pump suctioned seawater directly from the Pacific Ocean and delivered it into the catch basin via a filler pipe, where it followed the tunnels and canal to the aquarium/settling pond.

To reach the pump room, a contractor excavated a 104-foot-long tunnel during the summer of 1893. When finished, the room contained a steam-powered turbine pump capable of propelling 6,000 gallons per minute. In 1912, the steam engine was replaced with a 35 hp electric motor controlled from the powerhouse, which provided instantaneous water supply through the intake pipe.[42]

During the Sky Tram era, the tunnel was an attraction at Shipwreck Point, and visitors were allowed to descend into its narrow, dimly lit interior to the subterranean pump room. There, waves could be heard pounding against sealed-up intake pipes—a sound that provoked the chilling sensation that seawater might imminently flood the chamber.

The backup pump tunnel was sealed by the National Park Service in the 1980s for safety reasons.

Large Tunnel

In early 1892, Adolph Sutro signed a contract with James Schoolcraft and George Smith to dig a second tunnel through Point Lobos. Beginning near the northwest corner of the aquarium, the tunnel would run "in a northerly direction until daylight is reached on the North side of the rocky bluff." Still standing today, the so-called "large tunnel" extends about 200 feet from the aquarium to the north side of Parallel Point.

This tunnel had nothing to do with the elaborate waterworks of Sutro Baths. Its function was much

Large Tunnel

Aquarium/ Settling Pond

Powerhouse

more prosaic, serving as an additional source of rock used in construction of the Baths' foundations and for reinforcing the seawall and causeway to Fisherman's Rock. Many historic photos of Sutro Baths show ore carts on narrow tracks exiting the tunnel and running along the top of the seawall alongside the Baths. The tunnel also served as a convenient route for carts going the opposite direction and dumping rubbish on the far side of the point.[43]

The tunnel's last use came during the period 1955 to 1965, when it served as another attraction for Sky Tram passengers, who used it to explore Shipwreck Point.

Aquarium/Settling Pond

The aquarium began as a semicircular tank filled by water flowing from the catch basin. Over the years, its interior was subdivided and modified to serve as a settling pond for seawater being pumped to the Baths' swimming tanks.

According to historical newspaper stories, Adolph Sutro's original aquarium was described as 10 feet deep at the center, with walkways and steps cut into its sides that allowed visitors to walk around and examine the marine life trapped inside when the water drained away. Several details of this original

Large Tunnel

Aquarium/ Settling Pond

Powerhouse

Aquarium/ Settling Pond

The settling pond remained in use up through the last days of the Baths, and was repeatedly modified as newer technologies for filtering and pumping were introduced. By the 1930s, the pond had been compartmented with smaller concrete channels for diverting water. Within the pond, suction pipes and manifolds were installed to control the flow of intake water to the powerhouse.

Despite these additions, Sutro's original aquarium remains virtually intact today, although it has become badly silted-in over the years, and only about 75 percent of the original structure is visible.

aquarium function can still be seen: A large natural rock studded with seashells protrudes from the water, while a smaller rock is incorporated into the south wall of the aquarium a few feet from the larger one. Also, the concrete walls on the south and west aspects of the aquarium have seashells embedded in them in an attempt to mimic the appearance of the two natural rocks.

After 1892, the aquarium was converted to a settling pond for the Baths. Seawater entered through a sluice gate at the northwest corner of the semi-circular pond, where any seaborne debris was allowed to settle. The water was suctioned into the powerhouse via intake pipes, where it was heated and directed to feed channels leading to the swimming tanks. Unheated seawater was released directly from the settling pond into the feed channels through another sluice gate at the southeast corner of the pond. Varying the ratio of heated to unheated seawater controlled the temperature of the swimming tanks.

Powerhouse Ruins and Filtration Tank

The ruins of the powerhouse at the northeast corner of the former Baths area are easily identified by the concrete remains of the compartmented filtration tank, which looks something like a lopsided ice-cube tray. The powerhouse, finished in 1892, was the first structure completed at Sutro Baths. It originally served as a laundry and electric plant just for the Baths, but was substantially enlarged four years later when additional boilers and generators were installed to power Adolph Sutro's electric streetcar line.

In 1935, during a modernization, a reinforced concrete filtration tank was constructed within the walls of the original 1892 boiler house. The irregularly shaped, multi-compartmented structure held alternating courses of sand and gravel through which seawater was pumped and strained before draining out the bottom. From there, a series of valves allowed engineers to send the clarified water directly to the pools or into the powerhouse to be heated.[44]

The actual powerhouse structure was much larger than just the filtration tank. Its northeast corner is identifiable by the brick remnants of the smoke stack base, while the back wall literally left its mark in a concrete retaining wall on the north side, which retains the ghost imprints of door and window openings from the powerhouse.

Art Deco Tower Bases

When Sutro's received its 1930s makeover, the architects covered the original Greek Temple entrance on Point Lobos Avenue with an Art Deco façade that included two towers flanking the entrance doors. These concrete foundations were added at that time to support the spires. Originally painted in brilliant polychrome, the towers were remodeled once again in 1953 when the Whitneys changed the Point Lobos entrance to a redwood, Mid-Century Modern style.

Office Vaults

The Sutro Baths' management offices were located beneath the switchback staircase leading down from the museum level to the main promenade level. These two concrete-and-steel vaults, stacked one above the other, likely held cash receipts, account ledgers, and other valuables.

Diving Tank

Another surviving feature of Sutro Baths is the 1930s-era diving tank. Located immediately south of the old aquarium, its tall rectangular walls and remnant ladders make it the Baths' only recognizable pool. Because its walls were higher than those of the adjacent tanks, the diving tank is identifiable even when water covers the outlines of the rest of the pools.

Diving Tank

Other Pools

The brackish water that fills the ruins of Sutro Baths normally covers the outlines of the six remaining swimming tanks. However, their silhouettes sometimes become visible through the murk during prolonged dry periods; when the water level drops, it barely covers the concrete tank walls.

Wall dividing
Main Tank

Main Tank Staircase

Main Tank Staircase

A curved staircase cut into the rocky bluff near Fisherman's Rock marks the south end of the L-shaped main pool. This end of the pool did not have finished concrete surfaces like the other pools. Instead, Sutro used the natural rock of the cove as the southernmost edge of the main tank. This rock staircase provided access from the bathers' promenade to the main tank, and may be a remnant feature of the swimming pond that briefly filled the cove.

Main Tank Staircase

Refrigeration Plant

This concrete foundation with its subterranean vault stood outside the east wall near the grand staircase. A wood building atop the foundation housed the compressors and refrigeration equipment that kept the skating rink frozen. A window allowed visitors inside Sutro's to view the machinery at work. The cold was palpable even through the glass.

Refrigeration Plant

Refrigeration Plant

Sunbathing Patio

These broken concrete slabs are remnants of a patio built in the 1920s, apparently as a sunbathing terrace outside the west wall of the Baths. Nice days at Seal Rock Beach are infrequent, so it's likely that only the hardiest of swimmers used the area. After 1937, a locker room addition for the ice rink occupied the site. A causeway once connected the patio with Fisherman's Rock, but it was demolished as a safety hazard in the 1980s.

Sky Tram Features

The primary feature surviving from the Sky Tram's ten-year operation is the large paved viewing area on top of Point Lobos. Originally quarried in the early 1900s, it was paved by the Whitneys in 1955 and enclosed by curving cinderblock walls that allowed visitors to safely view Seal Rocks, the catch basin, and occasional fleeting views of the remnants of nearby shipwrecks.

Less obvious features include the upper waterfall, the filled-in trench that served as the loading platform for the Sky Tram, and brick treads and risers on Sutro's historic staircase leading down from the viewing platform.

Acknowledgments

IN THE MID-1950S, MY MOTHER, Doris Martini, discovered that Sutro's was the perfect place to while away long weekday afternoons with an active preschooler. Sutro's seemingly endless corridors and galleries were packed with everything needed to catch a five-year-old's attention: coin-operated nickelodeons, huge telescopes, squawking mynah birds, whirling ice skaters, and dust-covered mummies. As it turned out, the rambling building housing the exhibits proved equally fascinating to me, with mysterious doors and painted-over windows in all directions. I had to know what was behind them.

Thanks for getting me started early, Mom.

Sixty years later, when I embarked upon assembling the story of Sutro Baths, I quickly learned how little I really knew. This book could not have been written without the help of many friends and fellow researchers who generously shared their time, knowledge, and personal collections. I would especially like to recognize two who provided invaluable assistance with my research and writing.

First, I thank Ms. Marilyn Blaisdell, one of San Francisco's foremost historians and leading expert on Adolph Sutro and his wondrous Baths, for sharing her archive of photographs and documents. Many of the historic photographs in this book—including some never-before-published images—come from her amazing collection.

I also extend a special thanks to my friend Christine Miller, fellow historian and volunteer for the National Park Service, who has been researching Sutro's history for nearly twenty years. Christine provided me with a wealth of historic documents and news stories about Sutro's aquarium and the early construction of the Baths, saving me endless hours of research time.

I would also like to thank the San Francisco historians who answered numerous questions and provided peer review while the book was in draft: Tom Bratton, who worked at Sutro's as a teenager in the early 1950s; Jim Delgado, National Oceanic and Atmospheric Administration; John Freeman; Bob Holloway, National Park Service; Woody La Bounty and Dave Gallagher, Western Neighborhoods Project; Robert Smith; and the late George Whitney, Jr., whom I had the privilege to interview for the National Park Service; and filmmaker Tom Wyrsch.

Illustrations in this book come from a variety of sources, notably the fellowship of San Francisco historians and Sutro collectors who generously shared their photo and postcard collections: Jim Dickson, Wanda and James Fish, Dan Fontes, Glenn Koch, John Hall, Frank Mitchell, Dennis O'Rorke, Brad Schram, and Gary Stark of the wonderful Cliff House Project.

Local libraries and archives provided additional historic photographs and drawings, and I would like to thank their staffs for assistance both in ordering copies and securing permission to use their material: Debbie Kaufman and Mary Morganti, California Historical Society; Joan Berman and Kathryn Lasala, Humboldt State University Library; Amanda Williford, Park Archives and Records Center, Golden Gate National Recreation Area; Police Inspector Jeff Levin, San Francisco Police Department (retired); and Christina Moretta, San Francisco History Center, San Francisco Public Library.

I would also like to express my deepest thanks to the team who put this book together: Sam Stokes, publisher; Larry Ormsby, illustrator; Carole Thickstun, layout and design; and Susan Tasaki, editor and guru.

Finally, I send love and thanks to my wife, Betsy, who stood beside me and encouraged me throughout this wonderful, challenging project.

—John A. Martini
Fairfax, California

Notes

1. Robert E. and Mary F. Stewart, *Adolph Sutro: A Biography* (Berkeley, CA: Howell-North Books, 1962), pp. 184–185.

2. "The Sutro Aquarium," *San Francisco Bulletin,* September 5, 1887.

3. "The Sutro Aquarium," *San Francisco Chronicle,* January 7, 1886.

4. "Sutro's Aquarium," *San Francisco Morning Call,* May 14, 1887.

5. "Sutro's Scheme," *San Francisco Examiner,* September 4, 1887.

6. "Sutro's Scheme," *San Francisco Examiner* and "Sutro's Aquarium," *San Francisco Morning Call,* both dated September 4, 1887.

7. Reports, A. O. Harrison to Adolph Sutro (July–August 1889), California Historical Society, Sutro Papers Collection.

8. "Album of Sutro Heights," c. 1890. No publisher cited. Golden Gate National Recreation Area (GOGA)/Park Archives and Records Center (PARC) (GOGA 34879).

9. Drawing showing Sutro Baths c. 1891 (undated, no caption), San Francisco Public Library (SFPL) History Center, BP-49-281. N.B.: a nearly identical linen drawing also exists in the GOGA/PARC, George Whitney, Jr., Collection.

10. Report, Harrison to Sutro (November 21, 1890), GOGA/PARC, Sutro Papers Collection.

11. Classified ad, "To Architects," page 8, *San Francisco Chronicle,* August 5, 1891.

12. "Baths at the Beach," *San Francisco Chronicle,* August 5, 1891.

13. Drawing, Proposed Boiler and Engine House for Adolph Sutro, Esq.; October 1891, SFPL Blueprint Collection (BP-49-266).

14. "The Sutro Baths. Plans Adopted for the Establishment," *San Francisco Chronicle,* November 12, 1891.

15. Contract blueprint copy between Sutro & Ottewell Co., May 29, 1892, Bancroft Library (BANC), Sutro Papers Collection (BANC MSS C-B 465).

16. "At Sutro Heights. An Early Opening of the Bath-Houses," *San Francisco Morning Call,* August 20, 1892.

17. Letter, Little to Sutro, October 20, 1892, GOGA/PARC, Sutro Papers Collection.

18. Letter, Little to Sutro, October 10, 1892, GOGA/PARC, Sutro Papers Collection.

19. "Ready for the Water," *San Francisco Examiner,* September 18, 1892.

20. Letter, Hansbrough to Sutro, July 28, 1893. BANC, Sutro Papers Collection, Adolph Sutro Papers (MSS C-B 465).

21. "Saltwater Bathing for the People. Grand Opening of a Superb Palace of Water," *San Francisco Evening Bulletin,* April 7, 1894.

22. "Dashed to Death," *San Francisco Chronicle,* April 30, 1894.

23. "Adolph Sutro's War Whoop," *San Francisco Examiner,* May 14, 1894.

24. "The Sutro Baths," *Fresno Weekly Republican,* March 13, 1896. Article notes that "the building has been open to the public for several months, but the baths have not been used."

25. John Martini, "Merrie Way: Adolph Sutro's Forgotten Pleasure Grounds," *ParkNews,* Winter 2004.

26. "Sutro's Road. The Work of Construction Has Been Begun," *San Francisco Daily Evening Bulletin*, October 26, 1894.

27. "Sutro Baths Opening. The Big Building Was Illuminated and Tested Last Night," *San Francisco Call*, March 13, 1896.

28. Various San Francisco newspapers, March 14 and 15, 1896.

29. *Pacific Electrician*, November 1894, p. 37.

30. Unidentified newspaper clipping dated January 23, 1896. GOGA/PARC, Sutro Clipping Album.

31. Marilyn Blaisdell and Robert Blaisdell, *San Francisciana: Photographs of Sutro Baths* (San Francisco: Marilyn Blaisdell, Publisher, 1987), p. ii.

32. Forms, Sutro Baths Weather Reports (October and November 1896), GOGA/PARC, Sutro Papers Collection.

33. "Sterilizers for Bath Houses," *San Francisco Examiner*, September 23, 1900.

34. A. O. Baldwin, appraiser, Report, Estate of A. Sutro (May 1, 1910). Copy in GGNRA/PARC, Sutro Papers Collection (GOGA 18443).

35. "Fear Ocean's Fury Upon Sutro Baths," *San Francisco Call*, June 15, 1905.

36. Little documentation exists on the conversion of Main Tank, especially regarding the Tropic Beach area. However, historical photographs clearly show these alterations.

37. Email from Tom Bratton, former Sutro's employee, March 2013.

38. Interview, Doris Righetti Martini, September 1993, Mill Valley, California.

39. Oral history interview, George Whitney, Jr., August 13 & 14, 2002, Friday Harbor, Washington.

40. Ibid.

41. Interview, Inspector Jeff Levin, San Francisco Police Department, Arson Task Force, March 8, 2013. Inspector Levin graciously shared extracts from the 1966 San Francisco Police and Fire Department investigations.

42. "Pacific Service Supplies the World's Largest Baths," *PG&E Magazine*, September 1912.

43. Op. cit,, oral history interview with George Whitney, Jr.

44. F. W. Kellberg, Structural Engineers, San Francisco, Blueprint, Filter Tank for Sutro Baths (Revised 4-26-35). SFPL Blueprint Collection.

Index

Page numbers in **bold** refer to photographs and/or illustrations.

Photo Credits

Note that some of these images are copyright protected and others require permission to use; contact the appropriate individual or institution for specifics.

Appleton's Journal (July 16, 1870): p. 5

Marilyn Blaisdell Collection: pp. 4, 6, 7, 11, 13, 17, 27 (top), 39, 42, 52 (top), 55 (right), 59 (lower right/beige ticket, lower left/red ticket), 60, 65, 67 (bottom), 74 (lower right), 75, 76, 82, 83, 86 (top), 86 (left), 90, 101 (lower right), 103 (top and bottom), 105, 107, 108 (upper left), 110, 111

California Coastal Records Project: p. 23

California Historical Society: pp. 32 (CHS2013.1240), 33 (CHS2013.1242), 34 (top/CHS2013.1241), 36 (top/CIIS2013.1243, lower left/CHS2013.1244, lower right/CHS2013.1245)

Marc Cloutier: p. 2

Jim Dickson Collection: pp. 67 (upper left, upper right), 85

Wanda and James Fish Collection: p. 14 (#7, *The Golden Gate*, by Gilbert Munger)

Dan Fontes Collection: p. 106 (right)

Golden Gate NRA/Park Archives and Records Center: pp. 3 (GOGA 34879), 10 (Martin Behrman, SU-12), 21 (top/GOGA 34879), 31 (GOGA 2316), 50 (GOGA 13780.039), 72 (upper right/GOGA 35346 SSU-023), 80 (GOGA 18480.109), 87 (GOGA 13780.059), 91 (GOGA 35346 SSU-024), 104 (top/GOGA-3391-010, lower left/GOGA-3391 013, lower right/GOGA-3391 003), 109 (GOGA-3391 014), 112–113, 114 (top/GOGA 6467), 116 (GOGA-2316), 117 (GOGA-2316), 126 (bottom), 132 (lower right/GOGA-3386-005)

John Hall Collection: p. 46

Bob Holloway Collection: pp. 74 (upper left), 88 (upper left)

Humboldt State University Library: p. 27 (bottom/Ericson Collection/1999.02.0024)

Glenn Koch Collection: pp. 12, 34 (bottom), 52 (bottom), 68 (inset), 78, 89, 99

John A. Martini: pp. 21 (bottom), 118–122, 124–126 (top), 127 (bottom), 129, 130 (top), 131–132 (upper left, upper right)

John A. Martini Collection: pp. 48, 59 (top), 70, 77, 84, 88 (lower left, lower right), 101 (top, lower left), 102 (top), 108 (lower right)

Frank Mitchell Collection: p. 59 (center/blue ticket)

Lia C. Navarro: pp. vi, 1

Dennis O'Rorke Collection: pp. 81, 92–94

San Francisco Call: p. 30

San Francisco Chronicle: p. 29

San Francisco History Center, San Francisco Public Library: pp. 28 (AAC-0251), 35 (top/SFPL BP-49-184), 71 (top/SFPD Records SFH 61; bottom/Minnich SFP-27), 86 (upper right/Sutro Baths ephemera folder), 98 (AAC-0285), 102 (lower left/AAC-0243)

Brad Schram: p. 114 (bottom)

Gary Stark Collection: pp. 55 (upper left, lower left), 63, 72 (upper left), 88 (upper right)

Sam Stokes Collection: p. 106 (left)

This book was assembled in Quark using the fonts Dante MT, English Garden, and NicolasJenSG TT BoldSC.

The architectural illustrations represent a collaborative effort between the artist and the historian author. The artist developed 3D models based on records and photographs supplied by the author, including floor plans found in the archives of the San Francisco Public Library. After drafting the buildings in Adobe Illustrator, the artist then refined them in Strata Pro. DEM data was used to create the terrain, which was added in Vue. Most of the final renderings were developed from Strata Pro objects in Vue Infinity and finished in Adobe Photoshop.

Ormsby and Martini have collaborated on other detailed historical reconstructions, including 3D models of Fort Point, Alcatraz Island (present and 1867), Fort Baker, and the fort at Lime Point.

Printed in China by Amica.